Critical Guides to French Texts

9 Gide: Les Faux-Monnayeurs

Critical Guides to French Texts

EDITED BY ROGER LITTLE, WOLFGANG VAN EMDEN,
DAVID WILLIAMS

GIDE

Les Faux-Monnayeurs

Michael Tilby

Fellow and College Lecturer in French
Selwyn College, Cambridge

Grant and Cutler Ltd
1981

© Grant and Cutler Ltd
1981
ISBN 0 7293 0112 5

I.S.B.N. 84-499-5132-1

DEPÓSITO LEGAL: V. 2.704 - 1981

Printed in Spain by

Artes Gráficas Soler, S. A. - Olivereta, 28 - Valencia (18)

for

GRANT & CUTLER LTD
11 BUCKINGHAM STREET, LONDON, W.C.2.

Contents

Contents

For Susan

Preface

L ES *Faux-Monnayeurs* is a complex, and often elusive, novel. It may have an immediate appeal, and the main directions of Gide's thinking about his chosen genre may seem clear enough, but once the reader has accepted the invitation to consider more closely the author's treatment of the many questions of form and content with which the novel is concerned, he finds himself faced, not with a set of unambiguous observations but a veritable plethora of paradoxes, and no means of being absolutely confident of the validity of any interpretation or value judgement he may put forward. In the pages that follow, I propose what ultimately can only be *one* interpretation of Gide's novel. Yet, at the same time, I have tried to alert my reader to other points of view or criteria that may help him to come to his own conclusions. I have thought it wise to begin with a consideration of the various difficulties encountered in any attempt to make sense of the novel. The reader will then find, I hope, as comprehensive a survey of Gide's themes and preoccupations as the bounds of such a short study will allow. Finally, in Chapter 3, I have attempted to examine both the usefulness and the limitations of the various categories Gide himself introduces when trying to formulate the originality of his project. If throughout the book my principal concern is with the various processes involved in the act of reading Gide's novel, it is because of my conviction that this highly 'self-conscious' text demands an equally 'self-conscious' reader.

* * *

There is a readily available edition of *Les Faux-Monnayeurs* in the Folio paperback series published by Gallimard. All my references to the novel in the following study are to this edition. Except where otherwise indicated, references to the rest of Gide's writings are to the *Œuvres complètes,* edited by L. Martin-Chauffier, 15 vols (Gallimard, 1932-39), abbreviated *OC.* The italic figures in parentheses refer to numbered items in the Select Bibliography.

1

Introduction: Problems and Approaches

> Un livre tel que *Les Faux-Monnayeurs* se prête
> par essence à des interprétations qui sans doute
> sont des créations, mais qui épousent et prolon-
> gent certaines des lignes de force qui s'inscrivent
> dans l'œuvre elle-même.
>
> Gabriel Marcel

> Avant d'expliquer aux autres mon livre, j'attends
> que d'autres me l'expliquent... Attendons de par-
> tout la révélation des choses, du public la révéla-
> tion de nos œuvres.
>
> Avant-Propos to *Paludes*

> Mais, tout considéré, mieux vaut laisser le lecteur
> penser ce qu'il veut — fût-ce contre moi.
>
> *Journal des Faux-Monnayeurs*

L ES *Faux-Monnayeurs* was published early in 1926. It had
been conceived in a spirit of experiment and as such was
manifestly a product of its time. This was the age of 'moder-
nism', and Proust, Joyce and Virginia Woolf had already en-
sured that the novel was not to be outdone in this respect by
other literary genres. Gide was particularly sensitive to the success enjoyed by Proust's *A la recherche du temps perdu*, for it
had been as a result of his reader's report that the *Nouvelle
Revue Française* had turned down the manuscript of *Du côté
de chez Swann*. [1] With *Les Faux-Monnayeurs*, therefore, he was
seeking to make his own substantial contribution to the renewal

---

[1] See Gide's account of his dream in Proust's library, *1*, pp. 64-66.

of a genre that, with the loss of impetus by the 'Balzacian' tradition towards the end of the previous century, was widely felt to be in a state of crisis. [2] Though few would dispute Proust's superiority as a creative writer, Gide's novel likewise represented a striking departure both from the classic works of nineteenth-century realism and from the psychological novel as practised by the even then little admired Paul Bourget. And although experiments by more recent novelists have undoubtedly caused _Les Faux-Monnayeurs_ to appear in certain respects a surprisingly conventional composition, its place now seems assured in all serious discussions of the evolution of the modern French novel.

Gide had been born in 1869 and was therefore now in his fifties. He clearly felt it was time to take stock: _Les Faux-Monnayeurs_ stands as a _summa_ of Gidean themes, with its author attempting to pull together strands that hitherto in his work he had kept quite separate. (It is significant that his much admired autobiography, _Si le grain ne meurt,_ was written during the same period.) Within the compass of 500 pages, he introduces in a highly deliberate fashion a vast range of themes and preoccupations: sincerity (and hypocrisy) in life and art; justice (divine and human); religion (especially Protestantism); the Family; adolescence; homosexuality; illegitimacy; marriage; Freudian analysis; death; the problem of evil. The novel is also an explicit experiment with form, and much space is devoted within the novel to a consideration of the novelist's aims, the way in which his composition is progressing, and the alternative directions permitted by the genre at large. Moreover, the themes I have mentioned cannot be considered in isolation from the form of the novel, for much of their significance is conveyed through the means by which they are presented. A study of _Les Faux-Monnayeurs_ must, therefore, not only tread a careful path between formalist and thematic concerns, it is obliged to consider the complex relationship between the novel's form and content.

---

[2] See Michel Raimond, _La Crise du roman_ (Paris, Corti, 1967).

Les Faux-Monnayeurs was, its author felt, the only work of his that qualified for the classification *roman*. (Several works that he had originally designated *romans* were subsequently re-classified as *récits*.) This was partly Gide's way of recognizing that *Les Faux-Monnayeurs* was incomparably more ambitious than any of his previous projects. The scope of his novel and the intricacies of its structure were indeed such that the composition took him at least six years to complete. The record of his progress, as contained in his *Journal*, the *Journal des Faux-Monnayeurs* (published separately by Gide in 1927 and a necessary adjunct to the study of the novel), his correspondence and the diaries of his admirer Maria van Rysselberghe, reveals the composition to have been a laborious process involving much re-thinking of the original design. As he explained, 'C'est à l'envers que se développe, assez bizarrement, mon roman. C'est-à-dire que je découvre sans cesse que ceci ou cela, qui se passait auparavant, devrait être dit. Les chapitres, ainsi, s'ajoutent, non point les uns après les autres, mais repoussant toujours plus loin celui que je pensais d'abord devoir être le premier' (*1*, p. 56). It is clear from the early entries in the *Journal des Faux-Monnayeurs* that Gide was at that stage approaching his novel rather differently, and his hesitations are indicated by the fact that on two separate occasions he records that he has just finished the first twenty or thirty pages. [3] That Bernard's role was originally to be filled by Lafcadio suggests also that at the outset Gide's novel was going to be much more like his *sotie* of 1914, *Les Caves du Vatican*. He admits, too, that during the gestation of the novel, he was finding it necessary to believe that it was the only novel, and indeed the last book, he would ever write, since it was his wish that the novel

---

[3] There exists in the British Library an interesting manuscript containing an early version of Chapter 2 and part of Chapter 3. The differences between this fragment and the final version are considerable. Not only is this early composition much less succinct, it contains several characters who are subsequently dropped, and other indications that at the outset Gide had in mind a plot that was modified at a later stage. The manuscript has been published by Silviano Santiago (see Bibliography, *35*) but his transcription is not always to be relied upon.

should include 'everything', *sans réserve,* and should function
as 'un carrefour — un rendez-vous de problèmes' (*2*, p. 760).
He was in fact fond of claiming that *Les Faux-Monnayeurs*
contained the material for a host of different *récits.* (None the
less, he was to continue writing until his death in 1951, though
his work after *Les Faux-Monnayeurs,* with the possible exception of *Thésée,* points to a falling off in his creative powers.)
It is clear also that the composition was a highly conscious
activity, one the author needed to discuss frequently with his
intimates. The latter were treated both to accounts of his intentions and to readings of sections completed; their observations,
if not always acted upon, were certainly received with interest.
Roger Martin du Gard, whose *roman-fleuve Les Thibault* was
by this time well under way, proved so faithful a listener and
critic that Gide finally dedicated the novel to him. In many
ways, however, Gide's novel stands as a critique of the approach
to the novel exemplified by *Les Thibault.* That the two novelists
are, to a large extent, writing about the same *milieu* indeed suggests that, in creating *Les Faux-Monnayeurs* Gide was motivated, in part at least, by the desire to outdo his faithful friend in
a genre that for the latter did not require such radical innova-
tion. Thus, despite certain common preoccupations, the difference between the works of the two writers is considerable. In
the words of one reviewer, André Thérive, whereas *Les Thibault*
constituted 'une chronique puissante de romancier', Gide's novel
was 'une rêverie d'intellectuel' (*5*, vol. 22, p. 47).

Prior to *Les Faux-Monnayeurs,* Gide's essays in prose fiction
had been predominantly of two kinds, neither of which bore
much resemblance to the majority of novels produced either
then or now. On the one hand, he had created ironic, humorous
and playful fictions that he termed *soties* (*Paludes; Le Promé-
thée mal enchaîné; Les Caves du Vatican*) and in which no
attempt was made to provide the illusion of a plausible social
world. On the other, *récits* such as *L'Immoraliste, La Porte
étroite* and *La Symphonie pastorale* had revealed Gide's gift
for probing single-mindedly, and with a penchant for irony,
tightly circumscribed and problematical personal relationships.
In these *récits,* which have frequent recourse to the device of

letters or a diary, Gide establishes himself as the heir of a hallowed French tradition of introspection and psychological investigations, organized according to the dictates of a classical concept of harmony and order (cf. *La Princesse de Clèves; Adolphe; Dominique*).

At first sight, Gide's decision to turn to the novel is something of a paradox. As the comparison with Martin du Gard shows, his literary temperament differed appreciably from that of the conventional novelist: his interest in the external trappings of character and situation, which were still very much the novelist's stock-in-trade, was minimal. As a young man his leanings had been heavily in the direction of Symbolism, and as an habitué of first Mallarmé, then Valéry, he was encouraged in an aesthetic credo that had little time for a genre that so often had the appearance of a *pot-pourri*. (*Paludes* shows, however, that he was not averse to satirizing the Symbolist position. And in the *Journal des Faux-Monnayeurs* he objects to 'le peu de curiosité que [l'école symboliste] marqua devant la vie' (*1*, p. 53).) When, at school, he and Pierre Louÿs had drawn up a list of books for their desert island, they failed to include the work of a single novelist. Even after his 'Symbolist period', his relative lack of enthusiasm for the French novel is striking: when, in 1913, the *NRF* asked him to discuss his ten favourite French novels, he claimed that, had he not been restricted to novels written in his own language, he would have included only Stendhal's *La Chartreuse de Parme* and Laclos's *Les Liaisons dangereuses*. He deeply regretted there was no French counterpart of Cervantes, Defoe, Fielding or Dostoevsky. The talents of the French, he felt, lay elsewhere: 'Où la France excelle à mes yeux, ce n'est pas dans le roman. La France est un pays de moralistes, d'incomparables artistes, de compositeurs et d'architectes, d'orateurs' (*OC*, VII, p. 454).

Yet *Les Faux-Monnayeurs* does not represent a complete *volte-face*. For instead of converting to a set of practices that he had always rejected, Gide was setting out to endow the novel with precisely those characteristics the absence of which in the conventional novel had caused his indifference to the genre. His fictional novelist Edouard is heard to observe that, in contrast to poetry and the drama, the novel is a 'lawless' genre, characterised by its ability to absorb the most disparate material. Whereas other genres demand consideration in terms that are largely aesthetic, the novel is habitually conceived not as a creation in its own right but in terms of its relationship with external reality. [4] Therein of course lie its particular strengths, but *Les Faux-Monnayeurs* does not represent Gide's belated appreciation of these strengths. It was not that all of a sudden he decided to exploit the novelist's relative freedom from formal restraints. On the contrary, he made one of his foremost, if ultimately impossible, ambitions in *Les Faux-Monnayeurs* that of bringing the novelistic text closer to poetry and drama, making it in other words a self-sufficient artistic object. The means by which he sought to achieve such an aim consisted of the removal from the novel of all contingent detail and a persistent movement towards stylisation.

Moreover, it is important to remember that his scorn for the French novel was not total. His enthusiasm for Stendhal is, for example, particularly instructive. What he appreciated about *La Chartreuse* was that each time he re-read it, he had the impression it was a different book. The key, he felt, was to be found in Stendhal's lightness of touch: 'Le grand secret de cette diverse jeunesse, c'est que Stendhal... ne veut proprement rien affirmer; le livre entier est écrit *pour le plaisir*' (*OC*, VII, p. 451). When talking about the genre in general, he is indeed frequently concerned to show that his impatience is primarily with 'realism', and that in his view the tradition of realism is not co-extensive with the history of the novel. In the draft for a possible utterance by Edouard we read: 'Seul, le ton de l'épopée me convient et me peut satisfaire; peut sortir le roman de son

---

4 Cf. Albert Thibaudet, 'C'est que le roman, pour l'âge classique, n'est pas précisément un genre. Il forme au-dessous des genres une sorte de milieu commun, vague, un mélange, une confusion, dont l'essence est précisément d'être ce mélange et cette confusion. Il se définit par opposition au genre privilégié, le théâtre, tragédie ou comédie, dont le principe est l'unité et la composition, et qui ne souffre, lui, ni mélange, ni désordre' ('Réflexions sur le roman', *NRF*, 1 August 1912, p. 234).

ornière réaliste. Longtemps on a pu croire que Fielding et Richardson occupaient les pôles opposés. A dire vrai, l'un est autant que l'autre réaliste' (*1*, p. 54). A few years after the completion of his novel, he wrote to Martin du Gard:

> Il faudrait d'abord vous amener à considérer ceci: que le roman dit *réaliste* (au sens où vous pouvez l'entendre) n'est pas tout le roman (voyez *Pantagruel, Gulliver, Candide, Don Quichotte,* etc.) et que le genre roman, que la peinture de la vie réelle n'est qu'un département de la littérature (*3*, I, p. 468).

The examples he cites reveal, of course, his predilection for highly 'self-conscious' literary texts, texts, that is, which draw attention to their own compositional devices and remind the reader that what he is reading is pure make-believe.

There is much in *Les Faux-Monnayeurs* that shows Gide was in part harking back to a tradition of the novel that contrasted with the 'realism' of which he was so critical. Stendhal's influence may be felt in the treatment of Bernard, the authorial interventions and the casualness of the narrative voice. A second, corroborative influence was that of the English picaresque tradition; at the time he was composing *Les Faux-Monnayeurs* he was, in addition, engaged on the introduction to a translation of *Tom Jones*. He also stressed that his novel was written very much with the example of Dostoevsky in mind. In many ways, *Les Faux-Monnayeurs* is indeed rather un-French; not without reason did Martin du Gard describe it as 'matériellement, un *énorme livre,* un de ces livres compacts et pleins comme les romans étrangers' (*3*, I, pp. 274-75).

Through his widespread use of 'self-conscious' practices, Gide was also attempting to reveal that *all* novels are rooted in artifice. Thus one of the fundamental questions that have to be considered in a study of the novel concerns the extent to which it is a radiographic representation of the universal conventions of novel writing and the extent to which it is, more radically, an endeavour to turn the Novel into a kind of text that hitherto it had never been. In addition, since Gide encourages us to see his novel as 'une tranche de vie en profondeur ou en largeur', in contrast to the 'tranche de vie en longueur' offered by the naturalist novel, it has to be decided whether the move towards stylisation becomes an exclusive preoccupation *per se* or whether it can also accommodate the urge for a mode of realism 'superior' to that of Gide's Balzacian and naturalist ancestors.

Both on its appearance and subsequently, *Les Faux-Monnayeurs* has been much discussed, and the critical judgments it has provoked have been diverse. Leaving aside the many views that are openly partisan or moralistic — and Gide's stance on many questions of morality invites hostility from those of different persuasions (as Sartre has pointed out: 'il a su réaliser contre lui l'union des bien-pensants de droite et de gauche' (*37*, p. 85)) — we find that his experiments with novelistic form have produced in his readers reactions that are diametrically opposed. Whereas for some the novel represents a vigorous questioning of a genre that had by and large sunk into the conformity of middle-age, and advances an ever-youthful and liberating set of values to match, for others it has seemed pretentious, contrived and superficial, a self-indulgent exercise in Narcissism. That is not to say that all the judgments are so neatly polarized. Such phrases as 'brilliant failure' and 'demi-échec' are equally common. It will in fact be suggested in the course of this short study that *Les Faux-Monnayeurs* defies, even more than most other literary texts, a definitive, unequivocal assessment by the critic. For it is an ambiguous and paradoxical work that has the power to fascinate, tease and irritate. Much of its value may be found to come not from what it exemplifies but from its power to stimulate critical discussion. It is therefore by no means surprising that its readers have been perplexed or resort to formulae that can accommodate contradiction and ambivalence.

As so often with experimental works of literature, the differences of critical opinion stem from the difficulty of devising appropriate criteria by which to measure Gide's achievement. It will be seen in the following chapters that *Les Faux-Monnayeurs* is open to interpretation at many different levels. An element in Gide's text that seems gratuitous, flippant or heavy-handed in one respect may be an integral or appropriate part of it at another level. As critical readers we must guard against attributing to Gide aims that are either too restricted in number or inappropriately straightforward for a paradoxical novel its author has deliberately made elusive. For this reason, it is necessary to spend some time providing an accurate description of the novel's distinctive features before considering the various approaches to the text that propose themselves. This is particularly important in view of the fact that Gide appears to have given us abundant indication of what he was hoping to accomplish. So many of the comments made both in and outside the novel seem highly apt when applied to Gide's finished composition, and these will be presented in Chapter 2, but this does not mean that *Les Faux-Monnayeurs* is merely a realization of these ambitions. It possesses many features that are not afforded explicit mention by Gide. Yet equally vital to grasp is that by the very fact of being a completed composition, *Les Faux-Monnayeurs* presents its own complex logic, which is not reducible to the general and often vague formulations of Gide or his surrogate. It will be seen also that the novel is essentially a compromise between opposing and contradictory exigencies, reached with the aid of deft sleights of hand, and that often where it does appear to illustrate the ambitions shared by Gide and Edouard, the results assume a highly paradoxical status. Nor is this purely the result of Gide having as his ideal the almost impossible feat of writing a single work of fiction that is both an autonomous 'self-conscious' novel and a novel that exhibits in some way a superior naturalism or realism. For Gide's own position with regard to almost every topic raised in this novel appears peculiarly elusive and contradictory once there is any attempt to pin him down. The bent of his mind led him to a dialectical approach to all experience, and the whole of his literary career can be seen in terms of an oscillation between extreme poles. In this respect he closely resembles Ménalque, the hero of the youthful *Nourritures terrestres*, who declares: 'Je ne faisais jamais que *ceci* ou que *cela*. Si je faisais ceci, cela m'en devenait aussitôt regrettable, et je restais souvent sans plus oser rien faire, éperdument et comme les bras toujours

ouverts, de peur, si je les refermais pour la prise, de n'avoir
saisi *qu'une* chose' (*OC,* II, pp. 111-12). Much of his writing
— and his reading — is controlled by a mechanism that sees
the necessity for a corrective to an earlier contrary view or
stance. In respect of literary form, too, Gide can, more than
once, be seen to lunge from an open-ended 'self-conscious'
work to one that strives to satisfy what he saw as a 'classical'
aesthetic. His choice of subject-matter betrays a similar characteristic. For example, having explored in *L'Immoraliste* the
excesses of amoralism, he takes as the subject of the other half
of his diptych (*La Porte étroite*) puritanical self-abnegation.
Thus, in Jean Paulhan's words: 'Gide n'a de consistance en
aucun sens. Sur tous sujets, il a soutenu le pour et le contre'
(*7,* p. 158). Frequently in the writing of this *esprit critique* there
is to be observed a reluctance to allow a positive concept or
value to stand in isolation from its negative version. Ramon
Fernandez describes him, therefore, as 'menacé sans cesse, par
son démon critique, de perdre le réel qu'il avait reconquis, de
perdre son œuvre et de se perdre soi-même' (*15,* p. 51). If *Les
Faux-Monnayeurs* stands apart from the rest of Gide's work,
it is really only insofar as it provides a single stage for the
interplay of the many positive and negative aspects of his experience and taste.

Gide was also determined that his novel should not resemble
existing creations, but be considered 'assimilable à rien d'autre'
(*1,* p. 26). And indeed what is immediately striking about the
novel is precisely its strangeness. Though, as we shall see, this
is in some ways an extremely readable novel, there are certain
features of Gide's writing that demand from the reader his
undivided attention. And as likely as not he will still be dis-
concerted at every turn. For example, the vast number of characters, or rather the proliferation of fragmentary plots and the
brief indications of the relationships between the characters,
requires that he retain in his head a considerable volume of
information as he reads. The novel becomes a patchwork
of selected moments in a brief period in the characters' lives,
and plot no longer plays its central role. It thus becomes impossible to isolate a dominant narrative line. At one level, this

is the story of Bernard (with that of Olivier close on its heels:
some have identified the centre of the novel as the struggle
between Passavant and Edouard for Olivier). On the other hand,
it is Edouard who, despite his lack of achievement, comes
closest to being a central character, insofar as it is his behaviour
or personality that is Gide's most intimate concern. His resemblance to the author himself is over-riding proof that he is the
figure with whom Gide is most deeply involved. Yet, as E. M.
Forster pointed out: 'That is still not the centre. The nearest
to the centre lies in a discussion about the art of the novel'
(*16*, p. 105). As for the gang of counterfeiters, their activities
are kept, ironically and teasingly, in the background. Similarly,
it is impossible to isolate a single conclusion. In one sense, the
story ends with the death of Boris. But he is not a major character; he does not enter the story until the Saas-Fée section,
and the reader sees little through his eyes. He is simply the
helpless victim of external forces. And because these forces will
continue to exist, the novel must be extended beyond his death.
The final passage from Edouard's diary, with which the novel
ends, is no mere post-scriptum. His final words — 'Je suis bien
curieux de connaître Caloub' — remind the reader that in yet
another sense the ending is purely arbitrary. Life will go on.

The reader is further perplexed in the first section of the
novel by the changing perspective and the overall lack of a
sense of chronology. The impression given is one of disjunc-
tion and fragmentation. While, for example, Bernard is reading
an excerpt from the diary he has purloined from Edouard's
suitcase, we are at times aware of his presence, but for the most
part we are not. Predominantly, the sequence is experienced
with all the immediacy of the 'flashback'. The strangeness is
increased still further by the characters' tendency to talk about
events that happened in the past, rather than pursue a new
course of action. The past is thus continually confused with
the present, and although the novel is felt to progress in time,
each new present moment is surprisingly self-contained; in
contrast to the more fatalistic linear narrative that had traditionally been the basis of the novelist's art, the present in *Les
Faux-Monnayeurs* is never experienced as the culmination of a

rich plenitude constituted by a succession of past events. If this
has a disorientating effect on the reader, it is not so much that
the order of events remains hidden from him, but rather that
there is lacking a clear spatialization of time. Apart from the
innovatory impression of simultaneity that is on occasion required by this densely populated novel, there is the fact that
the reader is rarely given an accurate reflection of the distance
between a particular past moment and the present. Dates are
often left infuriatingly vague. In retrospect, it is possible to
create a structure of events according to a more conventional
sense of time. (Laura's pregnancy is, in this respect, of valuable
assistance.) Yet, paradoxically, establishing the chronology
brings the reader limited satisfaction. So often in *Les Faux-
Monnayeurs,* it is the immediate impression, duly recognized
as the product of artifice, that holds the key to a true appreciation of what Gide is attempting.

Not only does the internal chronology of the novel present
a curious impression, the reader is left in some doubt as to the
exact period in which events are taking place. (There is remarkably little by way of background, for Gide is not concerned to
emulate Balzac's creation of a detailed 'external' context for
the actions of his characters. Events take place in a world that
is the novel's own; even the external authority of the Law is
administered by judges who are also the fathers of those im-
plicated.) On the basis of a very few details given in the text,
critics have made some very different assumptions, and a little
space must be devoted to a discussion of the various dates
proposed. At first sight, the evidence seems to suggest over-
whelmingly that the action takes place before the First World
War. Gide himself wrote in the *Journal des Faux-Monnayeurs:*
'Si mon récit laisse douter si l'on est avant ou après la Guerre,
c'est que je serai demeuré trop abstrait. Par exemple, toute
l'histoire des fausses pièces d'or ne peut se placer qu'avant la
guerre, puisque, à présent, les pièces d'or sont exilées' (*1,* p. 23 ;
cf. p. 15). [5] The *faits divers* that provided Gide with his starting-

---

[5] His original idea was to divide the novel into two parts, corres-
ponding to the pre-war and post-war periods.

point (the student and anarchist counterfeiters, and the suicide of a young *lycéen*) were taken from reports in *Le Figaro* of 16 September 1906 and the *Journal de Rouen* of 5 June 1909 (reproduced in the *Journal des Faux-Monnayeurs*). Alfred Jarry, the sole undisguised intruder from life, died in 1907. Mention is also made of a bottle of Montrachet 1904. It might seem logical therefore to conclude that events in the novel are situated somewhere between 1905 and 1907. Yet a problem arises with the reference to Jarry, for it is clear the Argonauts' banquet takes place shortly after the première of *Ubu Roi*, the date of which was 1896. On the other hand, it is not just the 1904 burgundy that prevents us from assuming that the novel is set in 1896. In the opening scene in the Luxembourg Gardens, one of the characters is reading *L'Action française*, which was not founded as a periodical until 1899, becoming a daily newspaper only in 1908. (There are further references to Barrès, Maurras and the activities of the *Action française,* but they are too vague to be used to pinpoint accurately the moment of action.) So, if there is much to imply that the novel takes place before 1914, each of the different dates that propose themselves must in turn be rejected.

On the other hand, Armand's literary review publishes Marcel Duchamp's famous *Tableau Dada* of the *Mona Lisa* with moustache, a composition of 1919. Moreover, some have decided that the novel portrays, either literally (in which case Jarry's presence is a deliberate anachronism) or in effect, life in the 'twenties. As André Thérive put it: 'Sans la mention d'Alfred Jarry, pas un détail de mœurs ne ferait supposer que la date exacte n'est point 1924' (*5,* vol. 22, p. 42). And in a novel in which the impression is often as important as the reality, such a view expressed by a contemporary of Gide's must be taken seriously. Encouragement for this view may be thought to come from Gide's inclusion of the psychoanalyst Madame Sophroniska, whose name echoes that of Freud's disciple Eugenia Sokolnicka, who came to Paris only in 1921. (It has, however, been argued that she is placed in Switzerland precisely in order to avoid an anachronism that would be at odds with action set in 1905-07, a period in which Freud was still unknown in France.)

The strangeness of Gide's approach to chronology is matched by the unusual treatment of his setting. At first sight, the novel is unmistakably Parisian. The various residences are always given precise locations and are spread out over the more respectable areas of the city. When a character takes a walk, his itinerary is mapped out with precision. As a result, the setting has a concreteness that would serve well in a work of 'realism'. Yet in *Les Faux-Monnayeurs* little is as it seems, and paradoxically the city at times takes on an unreal, not to say surreal appearance, becoming an ambiguous realm somewhere between the Balzacian city and, say, the imaginary Bleston of Michel Butor's novel *L'Emploi du temps*. For the precise topography is never experienced by itself. It is the events that take place in the city that determine the atmosphere, and as everything we are shown is part of a tightly controlled world of Gidean symbolism, rather than a reflection of everyday life in the city, the impression is a strange combination of realism and the supernatural, familiarity and mystery. On occasion, of course, the impression of the supernatural becomes so strong that the concreteness of the setting is considerably lessened:[6] Bernard may encounter the Angel in the Luxembourg Gardens and be accompanied by it to the Sorbonne Church, but after that the route to the restaurant and the political meeting is not described. Once they have left the meeting, the topography becomes increasingly vague: 'les grands boulevards'; 'de pauvres quartiers, dont Bernard ne soupçonnait pas auparavant la misère'. As for the references to places outside Paris, they evoke a highly amorphous world. Germaine Brée has commented:

---

[6] That this was deliberate is seen from the following passage from the *Journal des Faux-Monnayeurs:* 'Il y a lieu d'apporter, dès le premier chapitre, un élément fantastique et surnaturel, qui autorise par la suite certains écarts du récit, certaines irréalités. Je crois que le mieux serait de faire une description "poétique" du Luxembourg — qui doit rester un lieu aussi mythique que la forêt des Ardennes dans les féeries de Shakespeare' (p. 69).

> La petite zone du monde réel qu'il occupe n'a pas de
> limites nettes; au-delà d'elle s'étend le monde, mais un
> monde obscur aux contours vagues, où vont se perdre
> définitivement certains personnages. L'Amérique de Lady
> Griffith, l'Afrique d'Alexandre et de Victor, la Pologne
> du fils des La Pérouse sont les régions frontières, inima-
> ginables, de ce monde où Pau, déjà, est un lieu d'exil.
> L'espace qu'occupe le roman, pour réel qu'il soit, res-
> semble au monde des Anciens: petit espace connu, plat,
> entouré de continents "mythiques" (*11*, p. 283).

A further perplexing feature concerns the identity of the
faux-monnayeurs of the title. Not only is the reader given a
long wait before he is introduced to the activities masterminded
by Strouvilhou (this is deliberate: 'C'est ainsi que toute l'histoire des *faux-monnayeurs* ne doit être découverte que petit à
petit, à travers les conversations où du même coup tous les
caractères se dessinent' (*1*, p. 28)), he gradually becomes aware
that the title is at the same time to be taken figuratively.
(Edouard had already decided to call his novel *Les Faux-Monnayeurs* before he became aware of the counterfeit coins that
were circulating.) It refers not just to the blatant insincerity of
a Passavant but to the inevitable falseness of all Art, as well
as to the way Education deforms Nature. In the end the title
becomes so widely appropriate that the reader is left applying
it at will and, in the absence of clear instructions from the
author, drawing his own tentative conclusions.

More problematical still is the precise significance of
Edouard. Just what is his relationship with Gide? To what
extent may we assume that his comments on the novel represent
his creator's considered opinion? Why does he fail as a novelist? What is the difference between his projected novel and
the text completed by Gide? What is Gide's attitude towards
Edouard's behaviour? To what extent is this the same as Gide's
attitude towards himself? Plausible answers may be found to
some of these questions but considerable uncertainty is bound
to remain.

Perhaps the most immediately disconcerting feature is the
tone of Gide's narrative. On the one hand, Gide is making the

most serious of claims for *Les Faux-Monnayeurs*. Yet the narrative, particularly in the first of the three parts, has a playfulness that has led some critics to complain of too great a resemblance to the *sotie*. (By way of contrast, E. M. Forster thought Gide was taking himself too seriously in his role as avant-garde theoretician and practitioner, being, that is, 'a little more solemn than an author should be about the whole caboodle' (*16*, p. 104).) The narrator or author (another problematical relationship!) is constantly intervening to draw attention to what he is doing or thinking, even on occasion protesting impotence in the face of the behaviour adopted by his creation. Related to this obtrusive narrative voice is the undoubted artificiality of the composition, an artificiality that becomes ever more apparent as study of the novel proceeds. 'Point of view' is another stumbling block. In a comparison with *Bleak House,* Forster wrote of Gide's novel:

> It is all to pieces logically. Sometimes the author is omniscient: he explains everything, he stands back, 'il juge ses personnages'; at other times his omniscience is partial; yet again he is dramatic, and causes the story to be told through the diary of one of the characters. There is the same absence of view-point, but whereas in Dickens it was instinctive, in Gide it is sophisticated; he expatiates too much about the jolts. The novelist who betrays too much interest in his own method can never be more than interesting; he has given up the creation of character and summoned us to help analyse his own mind, and a heavy drop in the emotional thermometer results (*16*, p. 87).

As if that were not enough, the highly conscious nature of the mode of composition employed in this intelligent and challenging novel leads to a text that never ceases to propose significance. At the level of both its irony and its symbolism, the reader will not always be given an authorial nudge, but once he is aware of this fact, he will find that there are remarkably few moments in the novel that give him respite from the vital task of interpretation.

There are, then, many features that make *Les Faux-Monnayeurs* a teasing and perplexing literary text. No less strange, however, is the fact that when reading the novel, we probably do not find it as perplexing as might be expected from the account I have just given. Paradoxically, it is only on subsequent readings that we are likely to realize all the ways in which the novel is unusual. In many respects it can appear quite a straightforward story, once certain constituents and practices have been recognized, and once it has been realized that certain other features expected will not be on offer. Individual scenes are outlined with great clarity, and there is an avoidance by Gide of any description of complex states of mind. This is, then, the first of many such paradoxes presented by the novel, and it is part of a wider paradox inherent in the relationship between the natural and the contrived that is to be found in any literary text. Equally paradoxical is the fact that if, as here, a novel is reduced as nearly as possible to its structural core ('le romanesque sans le roman', to use Roland Barthes's phrase), we are not left with what we feel is most typical, for we tend to think of novels in terms of their externals rather than their essence. Further analysis of *Les Faux-Monnayeurs* will show that it also subverts such oppositions as those that separate subjectivity from objectivity (Gide claimed: 'ces mots perdent ici tout leur sens') and form from content; in this novel each is an expression of the other.

The combined effect of these features is, from a traditional point of view, often singularly un-novelistic. For all Gide's skilful use of dialogue, characterization is perfunctory and deliberately functional, and the reader is thereby deprived of the opportunity to become emotionally involved with the characters. Likewise, he is left unsatisfied in his desire for background information. On the other hand, events occur that are reminiscent of a more melodramatic type of fiction (the surprise of Olivier's attempted suicide; the death of Boris). The novel is also full of improbable coincidences of a kind that serious novelists would not usually deign to employ. And by the terms of the traditional novel, the reader may frequently be tempted to pass criticism. Much of what he has come to value in the

Novel is not to be found in *Les Faux-Monnayeurs*. Yet it should be obvious that this novel cannot be approached in terms that are applied to a novel by Jane Austen or Balzac. To complain that Gide fails to deal adequately with the relationship of the individual and society, or that he does not give space to the Dreyfus Affair or its aftermath, is to miss the point.

Appropriately, however, the attitude towards deliberate artificiality in a work of fiction has undergone a change in recent years. Flaubert is now appreciated not so much as the master of realism as the key-figure in the evolution of a poetics of the novel that advocates a high degree of formalism as the means to supreme achievement. Similarly, there is now a much greater awareness of the vitality of a tradition of 'self-conscious' fiction, in which writers such as Rabelais, Cervantes, Sterne and many more recent writers derive complex and satisfying effects from flaunting the fictional nature of their compositions. Wayne C. Booth's now classic work of criticism *The Rhetoric of Fiction* (Chicago, 1961) has played an important part in disposing of the prejudice, fostered by nineteenth-century realism, against 'telling' in favour of 'showing', and no-one interested in 'self-conscious' writing can afford to be ignorant of it. As a result of this and other recent studies, it is no longer possible to dismiss 'self-conscious' literary behaviour as 'contrived'. Few would now accept, for example, Enid Starkie's observation, formulated in 1953: 'The intervention of the author himself, such as occurs in the chapter entitled *The Author judges his Characters,* is out of place in a novel in the first person.'[7] On the other hand, there is perhaps a danger that we are now too ready to believe that all 'self-conscious' writing is by its very nature imbued with a profundity that commands our respect. Many 'self-conscious' devices can be imitated superficially and to no significant effect. There is, moreover, by no means total agreement by critics as to the effectiveness of Gide's use of literary 'self-consciousness'. W. W. Holdheim, for ex-

---

[7] Enid Starkie, *André Gide* (Cambridge, Bowes & Bowes, 1953), p. 44.

ample, has written: 'In the *Faux-Monnayeurs* at last, the self-conscious novelist in his different incarnations or disincarnations... coincides with the problematical individual in quest of being, the Author as such becomes the prototype of Modern Man' (*21*, p. 260). Robert Alter, however, feels it suffers in comparison with *Les Caves du Vatican:* whereas Gide's *sotie* 'reverts, as most innovative novels have, to the underlying problematic articulated in the quixotic model of the genre', *Les Faux-Monnayeurs* is said to lack a dialectical 'doubling of character'. In Gide's only novel, there is, he says, 'too much direct playing out of fantasy versions of the self'. [8]

Much of the interest of *Les Faux-Monnayeurs* centres, then, on questions of structure and technique, but it would be utterly false to present Gide as primarily a theoretician. Despite appearances to the contrary, he was not interested in technique for its own sake. As Thomas Mann said of him, he was above all *un moraliste de race:* 'il eut pour lot l'inquiétude, le doute créateur, l'infinie quête de la vérité' (*7*, pp. 11-12). Yet Gide's starting point was always the self rather than external reality; he consciously explored questions directly related to his own state of self and frequently wrote in response to particular events in his personal life. Caution is obviously necessary in such matters but it would be foolish to deny that his fiction is often thinly disguised transformation of his own experiences. Thus, in rebellion against his Huguenot background — at school he was given the vulgar appellation *protescul* — and what was regarded as normal sexual behaviour, his writing was often undertaken in a spirit of self-justification, being an attempt to assuage feelings of guilt. He frankly admits, for example, that in more than one of his creations he was seeking to justify himself to Madeleine, his cousin and the wife of his *mariage blanc*. Like his fictional counterpart Edouard, he is the perpetual adolescent. He was concerned at all costs to 'find

---

[8] Robert Alter, *Partial Magic. The Novel as a Self-Conscious Genre* (Berkeley, Los Angeles & London, University of California Press, 1975), pp. 162 & 160.

himself', and probed relentlessly both the nature of his own
self and the forces that threaten authentic self-realization. The
means to authenticity he saw in a constant state of *disponibilité*.
For what he found within himself was an almost infinite number
of contradictions, which when pursued would compound themselves. (He once described himself as 'un petit garçon qui s'a-
muse — doublé d'un pasteur protestant qui l'ennuie' (2, p. 250).)
At one point in *Les Faux-Monnayeurs*, Laura says of Edouard:
'Son être se défait et se refait sans cesse. On croit le saisir...
c'est Protée' (p. 198). This Protean self was Gide's own. His
whole career was spent in finding an approach to life and art
that preserved intact all the feelings he felt were vital. Composition, therefore, inevitably became a dialectical process.
While wanting to remain open to all experience and embrace
extremes, he sought desperately to resolve his contradictory
feelings and ambitions in a harmonious structure.

These feelings did not always have their source in life. In
fact, Gide's was a world in which literary and, to a lesser
extent, philosophical texts provided nearly all the landmarks.
He would define himself with the aid of literary examples and
correct states of mind and feeling with self-prescribed courses
of reading. Once a friend of Oscar Wilde's, he too felt that
Nature was an imitation of Art. As the playwright Henry
Bernstein wrote of him:

> Gide a adoré la vie, mais souvent d'amour platonique.
> C'est un délice, pour ceux qui ont le goût des complex-
> ités, que de l'entendre maudire les livres, prêcher l'anar-
> chie, le départ!... Soyons libres, soyons modernes,
> s'écrie-t-il, et il nous raconte Narcisse, Philoctète, l'En-
> fant Prodigue ou Bethsabé... Et les démesurés, Whitman,
> Dostoïewski l'attirent. Il croit y rencontrer la vie. Ce sont
> des livres encore! Il se penche sur ces monstres, il caresse
> leur dos, mais seulement par-dessus la barrière. Il ne se
> résoud pas à sauter dans la fosse. C'est peut-être Pasiphaé,
> mais qui n'attend pas le taureau. Position délicieuse et
> ambiguë! (6, p. 34)

In other words, for Gide, the life of the intellect and the life of the emotions were fused as one, and much of the peculiarity of *Les Faux-Monnayeurs* may be explained by this fusion.

The importance of Gide's position in the history of French literature is undeniable. For several decades he was the grand old man of French Letters, exerting influence from the offices of the *Nouvelle Revue Française*. Even those who, like Sartre, claimed not to have been influenced by him had to recognize that they had grown up in Gide's generation: 'De même qu'un Français, où qu'il aille, ne peut faire un pas à l'étranger sans se rapprocher ou s'éloigner *aussi* de la France, de même toute démarche de l'esprit nous rapprochait ou nous éloignait aussi de Gide ... Toute la pensée française de ces trente dernières années, qu'elle le voulût ou non, quelles que fussent par ailleurs ses autres coordonnées, Marx, Hegel, Kierkegaard, devait se définir *aussi* par rapport à Gide' (*37*, pp. 85-86). When, four years before his death in 1951, he was awarded the Nobel Prize for Literature, the citation read: 'Pour l'importance et la valeur artistique d'une œuvre dans laquelle il a exposé les problèmes de la vie humaine avec un intrépide amour de la vérité et une grande pénétration psychologique.' But for Sartre it was *courage* and *prudence* that characterized Gide's work:

> Ce mélange bien dosé explique la tension intérieure de son œuvre. L'art de Gide veut établir un compromis entre le risque et la règle; en lui s'équilibrent la loi protestante et le non-conformisme de l'homosexuel, l'individualisme orgueilleux du grand bourgeois et le goût puritain de la contrainte sociale; une certaine sécheresse, une difficulté à communiquer et un humanisme d'origine chrétienne, une sensualité vive et qui se voudrait innocente; l'observance de la règle s'y unit à la quête de la spontanéité. Ce jeu de contrepoids est à l'origine du service inestimable que Gide a rendu à la littérature contemporaine; c'est lui qui l'a tirée de l'ornière symboliste (*37*, p. 87).

Yet it is difficult to imagine a similar encomium being written today. How is it that Gide's standing as a creative writer is no longer so high as it was? To a certain extent, this decline in Gide's reputation was only to be expected. It follows naturally from the type of response elicited by his life and work. Firstly, while much of his work may suggest a highly self-centred man, there is abundant evidence that he was appreciated as much for his stimulating company as for his writing. The theatre producer Jacques Copeau once wrote:

> Gide vous écoute parler. Nul n'est plus attentif, ne semble plus docile. Il suit mot à mot l'explication que vous déployez. La cadence de son chef balancé vous enfonce dans votre certitude... 'Oui', dit-il. Puis il reprend la question, mais d'un biais à vous faire avouer que vous n'aviez suivi que chemin battu; il touche un point que vous n'aviez pas aperçu, soulève un coin de voile dont vous n'aviez pas imaginé qu'on pût le saisir, délivre une évidence qui rend à la ténèbre tout ce que vous pensiez avoir accumulé de clarté. Et vous voilà dépossédé de vos raisons, vous promettant un peu tard de les mettre la prochaine fois par écrit, comme Sganarelle (*6*, p. 83).

Secondly, and much more important, Gide was appreciated as the agent of liberation. To homosexuals he brought considerable comfort: homosexuality is often present as a theme in his fiction, and in *Corydon* (1924) he stood openly as its courageous defender. More generally, his works provided the means to release from a stifling social and religious environment. A whole generation, it seems, responded to the call of *Les Nourritures terrestres* (1897): *Devenir qui tu es;* though, as in the case of the existentialist boom of the 1950s, it is clear many failed to appreciate the subtlety of Gide's message. Enid Starkie recalled: 'Gide me libéra des efforts désespérés que je faisais pour ressembler à mes camarades d'école. Il m'incita aussi à regarder en moi pour rechercher ce qui était véritablement moi-même, et, une fois cela trouvé, de garder intact ce noyau, de le protéger contre la fausse ambition, la suffisance personnelle, et surtout contre l'indulgence pour soi' (*7*, p. 42). It is obvious that once the social climate has changed and the constraints are no longer the same, Gide's writing will no longer be found so powerful in this respect. The appeal of his work was felt essentially by the young, whose needs necessarily differ from generation to generation. As Gide himself said: 'Les dispositions morales d'une génération ne sont point les mêmes que celles de la génération qui la suit.'

At the same time, it may be difficult to deny that Gide's work exhibits certain limitations. In the pages that follow I have chosen to place the emphasis on what seem to me the more positive aspects of Gide's novel, but it is clear from previous critical writings that recognition of Gide's achievements needs always to be tempered by an acceptance of at least some of the possible shortcomings I shall mention in my conclusion.

2

(a) *Gide's Starting Points*

IN the previous chapter, it was established that Gide was unwilling to work within what he saw as the principal tradition of the French novel. It is now necessary to look at some of his objections to this predominantly 'realist' tradition, before going on to look at the ways in which both Gide and Edouard seek to define their respective projects. Most of the general remarks about the French novel are made by Edouard, but what he says in this context is rarely, if ever, contradicted by the more specific ambitions that Gide set himself with regard to *Les Faux-Monnayeurs*. (A discussion of the relationship between Edouard and Gide will, however, be found below, pp. 43-48.)

At the basis of this shared attitude to the Novel lies an apparent objection to the genre's excessive concern with *mimesis,* or the representation of reality. The clearest expression of Edouard's basic position occurs during the conversation at Saas-Fée. He complains that

> le roman, toujours, s'est si craintivement cramponné à la réalité. Et je ne parle pas seulement du roman français. Tout aussi bien que le roman anglais, le roman russe, si échappé qu'il soit de la contrainte, s'asservit à la ressemblance. Le seul progrès qu'il envisage, c'est de se rapprocher encore plus du naturel. Il n'a jamais connu, le roman, cette 'formidable érosion des contours', dont parle Nietzsche, et ce volontaire écartement de la vie, qui permirent le style, aux œuvres des dramaturges grecs par exemple, ou aux tragédies du XVIIe siècle français (p. 183).

He expresses the view that the cinema has rendered redundant the novelist's pretentions to realism, and is adamant in rejecting Balzac's ambition to achieve 'concurrence à l'état civil': 'Comme s'il n'y avait pas déjà suffisamment de magots et de paltoquets sur la terre!' (ibid.). Rejecting the Naturalists' 'tranche de vie en longueur', he asks: 'Pourquoi pas en largeur? ou en profondeur? Pour moi, je voudrais ne pas couper du tout' (p. 184).

Gide's objection to *mimesis* is formulated more soberly:

> Le besoin d'écrire des romans n'est, il me semble, pas toujours très spontané, chez nombre de jeunes romanciers d'aujourd'hui. L'offre suit ici la demande. Le désir de peindre d'après nature les personnages rencontrés, je le crois assez fréquent. Il fait valoir un certain don de l'œil et de la plume. Mais la création de nouveaux personnages ne devient un besoin naturel que chez ceux qu'une impérieuse complexité intérieure tourmente et que leur propre geste n'épuise pas (*2,* p. 781).

The difficulty he found in breaking away sufficiently from this realist tradition is, though, suggested by an observation he confided to his *Journal* in 1921: 'J'écris, sans presque aucune peine, deux pages du dialogue par quoi je pense ouvrir mon roman. Mais je ne serai satisfait qui si je parviens à m'écarter du réalisme plus encore' (*2,* p. 699).

When we look more closely at the statements made by Gide and Edouard it becomes clear that it is not so much *mimesis* they object to as the techniques traditionally employed by novelists in the name of realism. They rightly claim that many of these represent, paradoxically, a highly unrealistic stance. Omniscience is a good example. The belief that characters have no secrets to hide from the novelist leads in Gide's view to an unnatural relationship between author and character. He singles out for criticism in this respect the practice of Martin du Gard:

> Sa lanterne de romancier éclaire toujours de face les événements qu'il considère, chacun de ceux-ci vient à son tour au premier plan; jamais leurs lignes ne se mêlent et, pas plus qu'il n'y a d'ombre, il n'y a de perspective. C'est déjà ce qui me gêne dans Tolstoï. Ils peignent des pano-

ramas; l'art est de faire un tableau. Etudier *d'abord* le point d'où doit affluer la lumière; toutes les ombres en dépendent. Chaque figure repose et s'appuie sur son ombre (*I*, pp. 29-30).

A related objection is directed by Gide against the dialogues that feature in a novel by X (again Martin du Gard?): 'La grande erreur des dialogues du livre de X, c'est que ses personnages parlent toujours pour le lecteur; l'auteur leur a confié sa mission de tout expliquer' (*I*, p. 32). And again, 'Le mauvais romancier construit ses personnages; il les dirige et les fait parler. Le vrai romancier les écoute et les regarde agir' (*I*, pp. 75-76). As a result, according to such a view, characters in novels are often much too consistent. Edouard notes: 'Inconséquence des caractères. Les personnages qui, d'un bout à l'autre du roman ou du drame, agissent exactement comme on aurait pu le prévoir... On propose à notre admiration cette constance, à quoi je reconnais au contraire qu'ils sont artificiels et construits' (pp. 323-24). It would have been entirely appropriate therefore had Gide followed his earlier inclination and used as his liminal epigraph Vauvenargues's maxim: 'Ceux qui ne sortent pas d'eux-mêmes sont tout d'une pièce' (*I*, p. 87). In the eyes of Edouard, and doubtless Gide's as well, novelists are also prone to say too much: 'Le romancier, d'ordinaire, ne fait point suffisamment crédit à l'imagination du lecteur' (p. 76).

Both Gide and his surrogate are equally clear at least as to the general direction their novels should take if they are to break away successfully from established practice. The true originality of their projects, as they saw it, lay in the essentially 'self-reflexive' nature of their proposed compositions, in their being, in Gide's terms, reflected *en abyme*;[1] as Edouard says, *Les Faux-Monnayeurs* will not have a subject: the central focus of the novel is to be the act of composing it.

---

[1] The fullest study of the technique of *mise en abyme* is to be found in Lucien Dällenbach, *Le Récit spéculaire* (Paris, Seuil, 1977). See also the article by Watson in *8*.

Gide's fascination with the use of mirrors in painting and literature goes back at least as far as 1893, when he wrote in his *Journal* the following, now celebrated passage:

> J'aime assez qu'en une œuvre d'art, on retrouve ainsi transposé, à l'échelle des personnages, le sujet même de cette œuvre. Rien ne l'éclaire mieux et n'établit plus sûrement toutes les proportions de l'ensemble. Ainsi, dans tels tableaux de Memling ou de Quentin Metzys, un petit miroir convexe et sombre reflète, à son tour, l'intérieur de la pièce où se joue la scène peinte. Ainsi, dans le tableau des *Méniñes* de Velasquez (mais un peu différemment). Enfin, en littérature, dans *Hamlet*, la scène de la comédie; et ailleurs dans bien d'autres pièces. Dans *Wilhelm Meister*, les scènes de marionnettes ou de fête au château. Dans *la Chute de la Maison Usher*, la lecture que l'on fait à Roderick, etc. Aucun de ces exemples n'est absolument juste. Ce qui le serait beaucoup plus, ce qui dirait mieux ce que j'ai voulu dans mes *Cahiers*, dans mon *Narcisse* et dans *la Tentative*, c'est la comparaison avec ce procédé du blason qui consiste, dans le premier, à en mettre un second 'en abyme' (*2*, p. 41).

A more precise description of Gide's ambition with regard to his novel is to be found in the *Journal des Faux-Monnayeurs:*

> Il n'y a pas, à proprement parler, un seul centre à ce livre, autour de quoi viennent converger mes efforts; c'est autour de deux foyers, à la manière des ellipses, que ces efforts se polarisent. D'une part, l'événement, le fait, la donnée extérieure; d'autre part, l'effort même du romancier pour faire un livre avec cela. Et c'est là le sujet principal, le centre nouveau qui désaxe le récit et l'entraîne vers l'imaginatif (*1*, p. 45).

During the conversation at Saas-Fée, Edouard enlarges upon such an enterprise. After various tentative formulations in which he contrasts reality and 'cet effort pour la styliser' or 'les faits proposés par la réalité et la réalité idéale', he finds himself coming to grips with his basic plan: 'Ce sera sans doute la rivalité du monde réel et de la représentation que nous nous en faisons. La manière dont le monde des apparences s'impose à nous et dont nous tentons d'imposer au monde extérieur notre interprétation particulière, fait le drame de notre vie' (p. 201). As in Proust's great novel, writing and the author's approach to experience become one. In the case of both Edouard and Gide, *Les Faux-Monnayeurs* is, moreover, to be a *summa* of the authors' concerns and a recipient for as many personal encounters and experiences as is practicable ('tout ce que me présente et m'enseigne la vie'). And as the formula 'un carrefour, un rendez-vous de problèmes' shows, the orientation of their works was towards the more problematical areas of human experience.

Such a project clearly represents a significant break with the practices of the nineteenth-century tradition. But, for all Gide's explicit and implicit criticism of *mimesis,* his project is still concerned with the representation of reality. His originality is to have refused to see representation in art as an unproblematical activity, and to have faced up to the distortion that is inevitably produced by all such attempts. And insofar as many of the features that Gide and Edouard hope will distinguish their novels are devised in response to a feeling that the techniques of realism are unrealistic, they become part of an attempt to produce what is in the first instance simply a more natural form of realism rather than a total rejection of its aims. Thus, out of respect for the way we necessarily experience our lives and those of others, the composition has to give the impression of being open-ended. The reader has to be given the feeling that 'tout n'a pas été dit'. Edouard wants his novel to end with the words 'pourrait être continué', while Gide says of his: 'Il ne doit pas se boucler' (*I,* p. 84). Similarly, the form of *Les Faux-Monnayeurs* has to accommodate the fact that 'la vie nous présente de toutes parts quantité d'amorces de drames' (*I,* p. 80). As Gide goes on to observe: 'Il est rare que ceux-ci se poursuivent et se dessinent comme a coutume de les filer un romancier.' Structurally, this means that 'chaque nouveau chapitre doit poser un nouveau problème, être une ouverture, une direction, une impulsion, une jetée en avant — de l'esprit du lecteur'

(*1*, p. 74). As a result, a great effort has to be made in order not to 'profiter de l'élan acquis' (*1*, p. 70). Perspective, as was seen from Gide's comments on Martin du Gard and Tolstoy, is vital. Hence the note: 'Ne pas amener trop au premier plan — ou du moins pas trop vite — les personnages les plus importants, mais les reculer, au contraire, les faire attendre. Ne pas les décrire, mais faire en sorte de forcer le lecteur à les imaginer comme il sied. Au contraire, décrire avec précision et accuser fortement les comparses épisodiques; les amener au premier plan pour distancer d'autant les autres' (*1*, p. 56). It is equally vital that the novelist avoid a single point of view; in a preface intended for *Isabelle* (1911) he had already declared: 'Le roman, tel que je le reconnais ou l'imagine, comporte une diversité de points de vue, soumise à la diversité des personnages qu'il met en scène; c'est par essence une œuvre déconcentrée' (*OC*, VI, p. 361). And during the composition of *Les Faux-Monnayeurs* he told Mme van Rysselberghe: 'Je conçois le roman à la manière de Dostoïevski: une lutte des points de vue' (*4*, pp. 34-35). Not that the Russian novelist was the only writer to encourage Gide in such experiments in perspectivism. He speaks approvingly in this connection of both Browning's *The Ring and the Book* and James Hogg's *Confessions of a Justified Sinner*.

Furthermore, the ideal towards which both Gide and Edouard were striving was an autonomous fictional world, one that appeared independent of its creator. This is how Edouard describes his practice: 'Si j'avais plus d'imagination, j'affabulerais des intrigues; je les provoque, observe les acteurs, puis travaille sous leur dictée' (p. 114). In reply to Mme Sophroniska he later explains that his novel has no plan: 'Vous devriez comprendre qu'un plan, pour un livre de ce genre, est essentiellement inadmissible. Tout y serait faussé si j'y décidais rien par avance. J'attends que la réalité me le dicte' (p. 185). In Gide's novel the protestations by the narrator of ignorance and impotence, and the manner in which he reviews the characters at the end of the second part, are all calculated to produce the effect of a fiction that, rather than consciously controlled, not to say invented, by the novelist, is constantly revealing itself to him, often causing him as a result surprise and even irritation.

It was seen earlier that in Gide's opinion the 'traditional' novelist did not show sufficient respect for the reader's intelligence and imagination. Gide is therefore determined that the reader of his novel should be made to work. Not only does he write: 'Je n'écris que pour être *re*lu' (*1*, p. 41), he concludes: 'Mon livre achevé, je tire la barre, et laisse au lecteur le soin de l'opération... Tant pis pour le lecteur paresseux: j'en veux d'autres. Inquiéter, tel est mon rôle' (*1*, p. 85). Similarly: 'Ce n'est point tant en apportant la solution de certains problèmes, que je puis rendre un réel service au lecteur; mais bien en le forçant à réfléchir lui-même sur ces problèmes dont je n'admets guère qu'il puisse y avoir d'autre solution que particulière et personnelle' (*1*, p. 24). An active role does not, however, begin only once the reader has reached the end of the novel: 'Je voudrais que le lecteur ait le sentiment qu'il [i.e. the novel] se fait devant lui' (*4*, p. 28). And far from being content simply to avoid telling the reader what to think, Gide feels it is appropriate to allow the reader to feel superior to the novelist himself: 'Il sied, tout au contraire de Meredith ou de James, de laisser le lecteur prendre barre sur moi — de s'y prendre de manière à lui permettre de croire qu'il est plus intelligent que l'auteur, plus moral, plus perspicace et qu'il découvre dans les personnages maintes choses, et dans le cours du récit maintes vérités, malgré l'auteur et pour ainsi dire à son insu' (*1*, pp. 63-64). As for the type of activity required of the reader, it is made quite clear by the statement:

> Je voudrais que les événements ne fussent jamais racontés directement par l'auteur, mais plutôt exposés (et plusieurs fois, sous des angles divers) par ceux des acteurs sur qui ces événements auront eu quelque influence. Je voudrais que, dans le récit qu'ils en feront, ces événements apparaissent légèrement déformés; une sorte d'intérêt vient, pour le lecteur, de ce seul fait qu'il ait à *rétablir* (*1*, p. 28).

Not all the prescriptions presented in *Les Faux-Monnayeurs* and related texts are designed to replace a display of omnis-

cience by perspectives closer to our own. An equally vital ambition for Gide and Edouard is that of giving their work an
aesthetic dimension they felt had hitherto been lacking in the
Novel. Their first step was to spurn the capacity of the novel,
particularly in its 'Balzacian' phase, to include the most disparate and heterogeneous matter. A similarity in terminology
reveals Gide and Edouard to be of one accord in this respect:

Edouard	*Gide*
Dépouiller le roman de tous les éléments qui n'appartien-nent pas spécifiquement au roman (p. 75).	Purger le roman de tous les éléments qui n'appartiennent pas spécifiquement au roman. On n'obtient rien de bon par le mélange (*1*, p. 57).

Thereafter the ideal was that of the 'pure novel', though quite
what Gide meant by the notion of purity is open to debate. He
accepted, however, that a totally pure novel was nothing less
than a chimera, and in the absence of a perfect model to emulate, he was obliged to derive inspiration from approximations.
Seventeenth-century French theatre was the best example of
artistic purity he could find. In the case of the novel, only the
English novelists of the eighteenth century — Defoe, Fielding
and Richardson — come anywhere near his ideal. Having been
forced, he says, to reject even Stendhal when considering French
novelists, he takes as his purest example of prose-fiction a work
that strictly speaking is not a novel at all, but a *nouvelle*: 'Je
doute pour ma part qu'il se puisse imaginer plus *pur* roman
que, par exemple, *la Double Méprise*, de Mérimée' (*1*, p. 59).
In the conversation at Saas-Fée Edouard, too, sees the pure
novel as the antithesis of the Balzacian model and the counterpart of French classical theatre. From what he says it is clear
that purity is, in his mind, closely linked with universality:

> En localisant et en spécifiant, l'on restreint. Il n'y a de
> vérité psychologique que particulière, il est vrai; mais
> il n'y a d'art que général. Tout le problème est là, pré-
> cisément; exprimer le général par le particulier; faire
> exprimer par le particulier le général... Je voudrais un

> roman qui serait à la fois aussi vrai, et aussi éloigné de
> la réalité, aussi particulier et aussi général à la fois, aussi
> humain et aussi fictif qu'_Athalie,_ que _Tartuffe_ ou que
> _Cinna_ (p. 184).

There is little indication as to how this ideal will be achieved
in a novel but it becomes obvious that this purity and universality would be embodied in a work that possesses an aesthetically satisfying structure and form. The formal model most
frequently proposed by Gide is taken from music, namely the
fugue: 'Nombre d'idées sont abandonnées presque sitôt lancées,
dont il me semble que j'aurais pu tirer meilleur parti. Celles,
principalement, exprimées dans le _Journal d'Edouard_; il serait
bon de les faire reparaître dans la seconde partie. Il serait dès
lors d'autant plus étonnant de les revoir après les avoir perdues
de vue quelque temps — comme un premier motif, dans certaines fugues de Bach' (2, p. 790). Once again, Edouard's ambition is couched in similar terms: 'Ce que je voudrais faire...
c'est quelque chose qui serait comme l'_Art de la fugue._ Et je
ne vois pas pourquoi ce qui fut possible en musique serait impossible en littérature' (p. 187). The fugue may seem rather a
lifeless and over-schematic model for a work of fiction — Mme
Sophroniska tells Edouard that she considers the _Art of the
Fugue_ to be 'le chef-d'œuvre de l'ennui, une sorte de temple
astronomique, où ne pouvaient pénétrer que de rares initiés'
(p. 188) — but for Gide it is a truly dynamic form:

> L'on ne sent plus là, souvent, ni sérénité ni beauté; mais
> tourment d'esprit et volonté de plier des formes, rigides
> comme des lois et inhumainement inflexibles. C'est le
> triomphe de l'esprit sur le chiffre; et, avant le triomphe,
> la lutte. Et, tout en se soumettant à la contrainte, tout ce
> qui se peut encore, à travers elle, en dépit d'elle, ou _grâce
> à elle,_ de jeu, d'émotion, de tendresse, et, somme toute,
> d'harmonie (2, pp. 705-06).

The extent to which a work of literature can reproduce a particular musical form is of course open to question. (See, for
example, _13, 23, & 31._) It should be remembered, however, that
a failure by _Les Faux-Monnayeurs_ to satisfy a rigorous defini-

tion of the fugue does not necessarily mean that the musical analogy has not been an important source of inspiration to the novelist in his search for an aesthetically pleasing structure.

b) *Gide and Edouard*

It should now be apparent that the area of agreement between Gide and Edouard is extensive. There is indeed much that authorizes us to see Edouard as Gide's spokesman. Edouard considers keeping, and then publishing, a notebook on the lines of the *Journal des Faux-Monnayeurs*. His Protean character is undoubtedly a reflection of his creator, as is his undisguised homosexuality and the preference revealed in his statement: 'J'ai plus de regard pour ce qui pourrait être, infiniment plus que pour ce qui a été' (p. 114). Both have difficulty in believing in their own reality — 'Rien n'a pour moi d'existence, que *poétique*... Ce à quoi je parviens le plus difficilement à croire c'est à ma propre réalité' (Edouard, p. 73); 'Je crois que cela vient plutôt d'un certain *sens de la réalité,* qui me manque' (Gide, *2,* p. 799). Edouard's attitudes towards the family and the privileged position of the bastard could easily be Gide's own. He discusses his novel with X in the way Gide discusses *Les Faux-Monnayeurs* with Martin du Gard. And when he thinks about the 'faux-monnayeurs' in his novel they assume characteristics reminiscent of the characters in *Les Caves du Vatican:* 'suivant que le vent de l'esprit soufflait ou de Rome ou d'ailleurs, ses héros tour à tour devenaient prêtres ou francs-maçons' (pp. 188-89).

On the other hand, Gide was undoubtedly keen to make a distinction between himself and his fictional novelist. He describes Edouard as a 'personnage d'autant plus difficile à établir que je lui prête beaucoup de moi. Il me faut reculer et l'écarter de moi pour bien le voir' (pp. 59-60). One idea he has is to make Edouard 'très désagréable'. In the event, the most far-reaching criticisms made of Edouard are those made by the narrator in his review of the characters placed at the end of the Saas-Fée section. Alarmed at the way Edouard has handed over Boris to his grandfather, the narrator sees this as an example of his character's fatal and irresponsible compulsion towards experiment. Edouard is shown to be unable, either in his fiction or in his daily life, to accept reality as it is. (Pauline claims he misses the important factor in every event to which he is witness.) His inclination is always to influence the outcome of events but without having any clear ambitions in mind. All this despite proclaiming that the novel should be 'dicté par la réalité'. This emphasis is brought out symbolically when Bernard (the realist) produces from his pocket a real counterfeit coin: for Edouard the counterfeit coin exists only as a symbolic abstraction, and he is forced to admit that he finds reality embarrassing. Edouard states that 'la lente décristallisation de l'amour' would be a fascinating subject for a novel but when he encounters an illustration of this phenomenon i.e. M. and Mme de la Pérouse ('la profonde désunion de ce vieux ménage'), he does not like what he sees. (See pp. 74 & 120.) The final demonstration of his cowardice in the face of reality is seen in his attitude towards the 'suicide' of Boris, a tragedy he had helped to create. He decides that the event will not be included in his novel. There is something outrageous about the trivial reasons he gives, all of which are designed, possibly subconsciously, to conceal his feelings of guilt: 'Je n'aime pas les "faits divers". Ils ont quelque chose de péremptoire, d'indéniable, de brutal, d'outrageusement réel ... Le suicide de Boris m'apparaît comme une *indécence,* car je ne m'y attendais pas' (p. 376).

Undoubtedly the most material of the differences between Gide and Edouard is the fact that the latter does not complete his novel. Gide makes it clear he never will: 'Je dois respecter soigneusement en Edouard tout ce qui fait qu'il ne peut écrire son livre. Il comprend bien des choses; mais se poursuit lui-même sans cesse; à travers tous, à travers tout. Le véritable dévouement lui est à peu près impossible. C'est un amateur, un raté' (*1,* p. 59). Moreover, the two examples of Edouard's work we are given contrast strongly with Gide's own mode of writing. Whereas his diary contains examples of an eminently Gidean style, the pages written under the heading *Le Régime cellulaire* and even more the excerpt Edouard reads to Georges are, it would seem, designed to appear grossly inferior to the various idioms perfected by Gide himself. Both passages are characterized by a rather heavy, moralizing tone and appear verbose when viewed alongside the economic style employed by Gide in this most skeletal of novels. Revealingly, Gide describes Edouard's behaviour during the conversation at Saas-Fée in ways that make him appear highly self-conscious; if during his attempt to explain his project he bustles around, pouring out tea or asking permission to fill his pipe, it is 'par grande crainte de paraître faire un cours'. In contrast, although the moral content of *Les Faux-Monnayeurs* is of supreme importance, it is Gide's achievement to have avoided all semblance of a didactic tone. The other salient feature of the passage Edouard reads to Georges is the distance from the everyday world implied by the use of the names Audibert, Hildebrant and Eudolphe; Georges observes: 'Eudolphe est un nom ridicule. Vous n'auriez pas pu le baptiser autrement?' (p. 350). In *Les Faux-Monnayeurs* Gide is concerned only to introduce characters who are recognizable as types inhabiting the society he wishes to depict.

In view of these significant contrasts between Gide and the character who so often appears his fictional surrogate, it may be wondered whether there is also a flaw in Edouard's theory of the novel. Several statements by Gide would appear to encourage such a suspicion: 'Chaque fois qu'Edouard est appelé à exposer le plan de son roman, il en parle d'une manière différente. Somme toute, il bluffe; il craint, au fond, de ne pouvoir jamais en sortir' (*1*, p. 54). And again: 'Rien de ce qu'écrit Edouard, n'est, à mes yeux, parfaitement juste, parfaitement exact. Il entre dans chacune de ses réflexions ce léger biais qui fait que c'est Edouard qui la pense, et non moi' (*3*, I, p. 281). Yet it is difficult to isolate a single artistic belief or ambition expressed by Edouard that is at variance with Gide's own position. His shortcomings would appear to be exclusively in his practice. None the less, such a conclusion is premature if there has been no discussion of the reception given Edouard's ideas on the novel expounded at Saas-Fée.

It might be thought that Edouard's ideas come off rather badly here. Both Madame Sophroniska and Laura gently mock his project. Edouard himself is made to feel 'l'inconvenance et l'outrance et l'absurdité' (p. 182) of his words, and afterwards he reflects that his opinions and ambitions were nothing but *âneries*. More devastating perhaps is a comment by the narrator accusing Edouard of contradicting himself; 'L'illogisme de son propos était flagrant, sautait aux yeux d'une manière pénible. Il apparaissait clairement que, sous son crâne, Edouard abritait deux exigences inconciliables, et qu'il s'usait à les vouloir accorder' (p. 186). Let us take these points in turn. We should not, I think, pay too much heed to the reaction of the two women. Neither represents an authoritative position in such matters. Gide, after all, does not find Bach boring! As much as anything, they are responding to Edouard's diffidence and embarrassment; they sense his vulnerability and enjoy deflating him. The difference between Gide and Edouard in this question of theory is, I would suggest, not conceptional but a matter of personality and tone. If Edouard is made to appear ridiculous, it is as a result of his slightly pompous and pretentious manner. It is made quite clear that he is out to impress Bernard and as such is unable to behave as naturally as Gide would like; he is in fact unable to resist the temptation to deliver a lecture. Totally absent is the degree of self-directed irony that Gide seems to regard as a prerequisite for sincerity. Edouard's retrospective irritation with himself is, however, evidence that, like the more attractive of the adolescents in the novel, he always knows when he has been playing a role. What, though, of the charge of illogicality? It appears utterly justified. A novel cannot at one and the same time be dictated by reality and obey fully the dictates of stylization. Yet this is precisely what Gide is attempting in *Les Faux-Monnayeurs*. And we are, I think, obliged to conclude that the existence of a fundamental contradiction in Edouard's ambition does not necessarily invalidate that ambition as far as Gide himself is concerned. Edouard's problem is that he cannot devise a way of accommodating this contradiction within a compositional structure. If Gide is successful, it is because, as we shall see, he contrives a work of multiple paradox, one that makes constant play of contrasts between appearances and reality.

What I am suggesting is that the somewhat negative response to Edouard's discourse on the novel he wishes to write can be a little misleading. It should not, I think, be taken to imply, as Gide himself suggested to Martin du Gard, a significant degree of dissatisfaction with Edouard's views on the ideal novel. What separates Edouard from Gide is, first of all, his personality, however similar the two figures may seem at times, and, more importantly, his failure to move beyond the realm of theory into the sphere of practice, and his equivocal attitude to the reality he claims to respect. Yet when all is said and done, the precise nature of the distinction between the two figures will inevitably remain blurred. For instead of starting with a programmed account of the differences between Edouard and his creator, Gide, like many another writer, sees his character developing according to the needs of the novel, responding more or less spontaneously to the situation in which he is placed. Once inserted in a fiction, a character will always distort any model the author may have taken, even if the latter is attempting a faithful reproduction. What Gide finds when he contemplates those characters who have close affinities with himself is that they exaggerate certain tendencies he detects in his own character: 'Ce qui manque à chacun de mes héros, que j'ai taillés dans ma chair même, c'est ce peu de bon sens qui me retient de pousser aussi loin qu'eux leurs folies' (*I*, p. 73). He was also right to tell Martin du Gard that Edouard's diary was much more of a novel than the author of *Les Thibault* had supposed. That he was concerned to direct our attention to the various degrees discernible in the relationship between the author and his created character is underlined by the presence of the chapter from Edouard's novel which shows Audibert facing a situation analogous to that of Edouard himself. Audibert's conversation is clinical and detached. Unlike Edouard, he has no personality. The faintly absurd name with which he is blessed hints at Gide's intention to show how easily the fictional character appears as a parody of the creator's own self. The *mise en abyme* takes Gide and the reader into ever widening areas of distortion, a multiplication of differences separating characters from the original authorial self they still resemble. *Les Faux-Monnayeurs* is, in this respect, truly an example of what Michel Butor has termed *le roman comme recherche*. Gide discovers through his composition just how mysterious are the complex phenomena proposed by the creative imagination. Although by virtue of being *relational* they lend themselves to a certain degree of rationalization, they end up presenting an ever-shifting pattern that is indicative and suggestive rather than a definition or solution.

Perhaps it should be added that although the relationship between Edouard and Gide is necessarily elusive, it may be that Gide finds this a convenient way of avoiding the task of thinking through the questions raised by the inclusion of a character who bears such a strong resemblance to himself. Claude-Edmonde Magny, for example, claims: 'Il a tâché de prévenir toute identification entre Edouard et lui, précisément parce qu'il voulait pouvoir en faire une sorte de bouc émissaire; enfin, il s'est ménagé une porte de sortie au cas où la tentative du roman pur se présenterait comme plus viable qu'il ne semblait d'abord' (*29*, p. 221). In other words, it seems possible to view the uncertainty that surrounds the relationship of Edouard to Gide as both inevitable *and* a sign that Gide was glossing over questions that did in fact invite a more rigorous treatment. It will be seen later that many other features of Gide's novel lend themselves to both a positive and negative interpretation. Certainly, one of the most difficult to rebut of the charges levelled against the author of *Les Faux-Monnayeurs* is the one which sees him turning his major weaknesses into minor strengths.

(c) *Themes*

The setting of Gide's novel also constitutes one of his main themes. For, in addition to his other aims, Gide sought to present in *Les Faux-Monnayeurs* an indictment of contemporary society, or to be more precise, an indictment of those *milieux* with which he was personally acquainted. What we find in his novel is essentially the world of the professions swelled by the inclusion of examples of, ostensibly, the more respectable kind of intellectual and artist, and by representatives of the Protestant clergy, whose church had been an important but not always welcome influence on Gide's upbringing. His particular concern was to make apparent the falseness he detected everywhere in that society, and without ever seeking to be subtle, he makes frequent use of satire to that end. The novel also provided him with an opportunity to explore a question that had always been one of his closest concerns: the individual's attempt to find his true self, and the constraints and opposition he meets in the process. Most of Gide's characters are engaged in some kind of self-examination [2] (not always voluntarily) but it is the adolescent who is best suited to his purpose. The adolescent's freshness of approach, his openness to experience and his relative naivety emphasize by contrast the moral stagnation that in Gide's eyes constitutes the norm in the adult world. There was, moreover, a profound bond between Gide and the male adolescent. The latter was *un être en formation,* and Gide was naturally drawn to the future rather than the present or past, epochs that an earlier adolescent, Chateaubriand's René, had already dismissed as 'deux statues incomplètes' — 'L'une a été retirée toute mutilée du débris des âges; l'autre n'a pas encore reçu sa perfection de l'avenir.' How right Ramon Fernandez was when he described Gide as an 'éternel adolescent, éternel débutant, mais doué d'une pénétration et d'une méfiance que la jeunesse ignore' (*15,* p. 30)!

In the world of *Les Faux-Monnayeurs* natural behaviour is seen to be almost impossible. Most of the characters are haunted by secret feelings of guilt, many of which are sexual in origin: illegitimacy, adultery, masturbation, homosexuality, syphilis, sexual activity involving minors. Even those, such as Rachel or Mélanie Vedel, whose conduct is irreproachable, may still try to conceal from outsiders the nature of their situation. And it is often these secrets that bind characters to each other. A crude and ironic reflection of the moral decay that holds society together can be seen in the compromising documents that each *faux-monnayeur* has to provide. ('Il faut que les gosses se compromettent et qu'ils livrent de quoi tenir les

---

[2] The name of Hamlet recurs frequently in Gide's writings.

parents' (p. 260).) As the cynical Strouvilhou explains to Ghéridanisol: 'Il est bon ... il est même indispensable de créer
des rapports de réciprocité entre les citoyens; c'est ainsi que
se forment les sociétés solides. On se tient, quoi! Nous tenons
les petits, qui tiennent leurs parents, qui nous tiennent. C'est
parfait' (p. 261). There is not a single character who is prepared
to be frank at all times. In Germaine Brée's words: 'Tous les
personnages du roman, bon gré, mal gré, sont par moments
des faux-monnayeurs' (*11,* p. 293). However, the unnatural
behaviour of Gide's characters does not come purely from
their need to suppress certain truths about their nature or their
past behaviour. Falseness, deception and hypocrisy are rampant
on a much wider scale. No reader of *Les Faux-Monnayeurs* can
fail to notice the novel's most blatant examples of hypocrisy.
The most obvious counterfeit figure is the aristocrat Passavant,
both in the realm of art — 'Les convictions artistiques dont il
fait montre, ne s'affirment si véhémentes que parce qu'elles
ne sont pas profondes; nulle secrète exigence de tempérament
ne les commande; elles répondent à la dictée de l'époque;
leur mot d'ordre est: opportunité' (p. 76) — and on most of
the other occasions on which we see him. [3] Lady Griffith, who,
incidentally, appears to appreciate Passavant precisely for his
falseness, treats him to a candid portrayal of himself when she
says: 'Vous avez toutes les qualités de l'homme de lettres:
vous êtes vaniteux, hypocrite, ambitieux, versatile, égoïste'
(p. 50). She knows he is incapable of being sincere, and tells
him that any attempt by him to blush would be a waste of
time. Yet she herself is open to similar castigation for her
treatment of Vincent. (Although we are obviously meant to
recoil from Passavant's behaviour, Gide does strike a slightly
different note when he has him describe his attitude to his
father's death. What Passavant says may not endear him to us
— contrast Gontran's more warm-hearted reaction — but is he
not at least being frank on this occasion? After all, Camus's

---

[3] 'Sa monnaie émise par la vanité s'adresse à la vanité et ne donne
le change à personne' (*11,* p. 293). He is also accused of plagiarism
and is marked out by his relationship with Strouvilhou.

hero Meursault was later to be regarded as admirably honest when on a similar occasion he refused to feign the emotion expected of him.)

Perhaps even more insidious than the calculating hypocrisy of Gide's villains, though, is the unconscious falseness or hypocrisy which is often set before us. As the narrator says with reference to Edouard's decision to bring Boris back to Paris: 'Pourquoi cherche-t-il à se persuader, à présent, qu'il conspire au bien de Boris? Mentir aux autres, passe encore; mais à soi-même!' (p. 216). Oscar Molinier is another who is conveniently unaware of the discrepancy between his precepts and his actions, the similarity between his own situation and situations he openly criticizes when they involve others. Indeed, it might be said that his character is decidedly one-dimensional, a constant demonstration of the startling degree of self-deception that can be exhibited by a professional judge of other men's faults. A more or less unconscious hypocrisy is also apparent in Laura's decision to marry Douviers, in Douviers's shortlived promise of forgiveness, in the behaviour of M. and Mme de la Pérouse, though in their case it is complicated by the suggestion of very real paranoia. How quickly, too, Profitendieu's 'paternal' devotion to Bernard is lost from sight when Edouard mentions the false coin Bernard had shown him at Saas-Fée!

The source of much of this behaviour is the Pension Azaïs-Vedel, so much so that Mme Brée, ironically recalling 'la maison Vauquer' in Balzac's *Le Père Goriot,* has written: 'Le centre réel d'émission de fausse monnaie, celui qui intéresse avant tout Gide c'est la pension Azaïs; Strouvilhou, qui l'a fréquentée, n'en est qu'un sous-produit. Les itinéraires de tous les personnages principaux passent par la pension Azaïs. Elle est le Vatican des *Faux-Monnayeurs'* (*11*, p. 294). Vedel's hypocrisy is subtly revealed, first by Edouard and Sarah and then by Armand, who says: 'Quant à papa, il s'en remet au Seigneur; c'est plus commode' (p. 239). Azaïs, whose presence is felt even more strongly than that of his son, conveniently refuses to accept even the possibility of immorality in his orbit. His blindness has a cruelly ironic effect on those for whom he should

fulfil the role of spiritual guide. Edouard, having described him
charitably as *une âme simple,* observes: 'Dès qu'on est un peu
moins simple soi-même, on est contraint, en face d'elles [i.e.
the *âmes simples*], à une espèce de comédie; peu honnête;
mais qu'y faire? On ne peut discuter, mettre au point; on
est contraint d'acquiescer. Azaïs impose autour de lui l'hypo-
crisie, pour peu qu'on ne partage pas sa croyance' (p. 106).
The *pension* is therefore a hot-house, in which lies, deception
and cynicism flourish, and, as the example of Armand shows,
this behaviour can even become the basis of a perverse enjoy-
ment. Yet it would be misleading to identify hypocrisy only
with the effects of a Protestant education. Oscar Molinier is
not a Protestant, and Gide leaves it quite clear that bourgeois
society as a whole is ridden with the falseness he abhors.

In many of these cases, the unconscious hypocrisy is revealed to us through irony rather than through direct narratorial
commentary. Moreover, with a characteristic eye to variety and
the gradations that respect the fine dividing-line between related
sentiments, Gide includes examples in which sincerity is seemingly questioned without hypocrisy being firmly established in
its place. The reader is left to wonder, for example, how Charles
Profitendieu views the conversation he is having with his father
at the end of the second chapter. Similarly, it is impossible to
know whether Edouard's courtship of Laura was undertaken
in bad faith or in genuine ignorance of (or uncertainty about)
his true sexual orientation. Gide is, on more than one occasion,
careful to leave the reader's curiosity unsatisfied.

Yet another interesting case is provided by Armand Vedel.
For, in contrast to 'the *bons bourgeois* of *Les Faux-Monnayeurs*
who are totally unaware of the atmosphere of hypocrisy and
falsified feelings which is their natural environment', as J. C.
Davies puts it (*8,* p. 134), he recognizes the hypocrisy of his
behaviour and indeed revels in it. As well as recalling certain
heroes of Dostoevsky, Armand is, loosely speaking, a Baude-
lairean figure — it is no coincidence that he chooses an epigraph
from *Les Fleurs du mal* for his crudely titled review *Le Vase
nocturne,* or that it is taken from the poem 'L'Amour du men-
songe'. His characteristic activity is that of self-vilification: 'Je

sais que je ne suis qu'un salaud ; et je n'ai jamais cherché à poser pour autre chose' (p. 239). Bernard sees him as *contrefait* and notes : 'Son esprit n'est appliqué qu'à détruire ; du reste, c'est contre lui-même qu'il se montre le plus acharné ; tout ce qu'il a de bon en lui, de généreux, de noble ou de tendre, il en prend honte' (p. 253). His honesty makes it impossible for him to ignore the hypocrisy around him, and as such he is extremely useful to Gide ; it is Armand who observes : 'Comme si chacun de nous ne jouait pas, plus ou moins sincèrement et consciemment. La vie, mon vieux, n'est qu'une comédie' (p. 356). But he is not given the strength to achieve a genuine moral superiority. Depressed by the climate in which he lives he can only imitate and declare his difference in terms of a greater self-awareness. Consistently perverse, his only pleasure comes from acting as a gross caricature of his fellow men, consciously outdoing them in the characteristics he despises. Or, as in his attitude towards Sarah, encouraging a person in a bold or daring act, only to judge them afterwards with particular severity. Such behaviour is entirely in keeping with his self-loathing, but he is not always able to carry out his role with such aplomb. At one point Olivier detects the words catching in Armand's throat and notices the *accent pathétique* of his voice. Earlier, he had been anxious that Edouard should not receive the wrong impression of his friend :

> C'est une espèce de rôle qu'il joue ... malgré lui. Au fond il est très différent de cela... Je ne peux pas vous expliquer. Il a une espèce de besoin d'abîmer tout ce à quoi il tient le plus. Il n'y a pas longtemps qu'il est comme ça. Je crois qu'il est très malheureux et que c'est pour cacher cela qu'il se moque. Il est très fier. Ses parents ne le comprennent pas du tout. Ils voulaient en faire un pasteur (p. 112).

This unhappiness is indeed powerfully revealed in his actions with the bloodstained handkerchief. Although Armand's role in the events of the novel is a relatively modest one, his enigmatic character may easily be found one of the most fascinating.

Small wonder therefore that Strouvilhou is led to observe:
'Dans un monde où chacun triche, c'est l'homme vrai qui fait
figure de charlatan' (p. 319). All in all, society is viewed as an
unwholesome environment, and the effect on the young is
correspondingly one of contamination. Paris is a constant zone
of temptation. (Africa and the colonies have the function of a
place of perdition.) Both the children and the adolescents are
corrupted. It is not just a matter of their 'posing'. Nor is it
simply a question of immoral or criminal activities. But rather
that, to a greater or lesser extent, their behaviour is always
characterized by deceit and lying. Locked drawers are broken
into, private diaries and letters read. Not even the well-mean-
ing Bernard is immune from the temptation to indulge in such
activities.

As Edouard remarks with reference to society, 'la forêt
façonne l'arbre. A chacun, si peu de place est laissée!' (p. 268).
The society in which he lives is stifling, and it is significant
that the novel abounds in images of suffocation. Apart from
the explicit allusion to the spiritual atmosphere of the *pension*,
reference is made to the oppressive summer heat, the fetid
atmosphere of rooms, which are also often depicted as smoke-
filled. Olivier's chosen means of suicide is suffocation by gas.
Correspondingly, much play is made of the need for fresh air
and open windows. In such a world healthy development is
seen as well-nigh impossible. In Germaine Brée's words: 'La
société, faux-monnayeur essentiel du roman, tend à imposer
à l'individu une forme stéréotypée qui n'est pas la sienne'
(*11,* p. 309).

This, then, is the setting for the principal quest in the novel:
Bernard's epic journey in search of authenticity. (The modest
proportions of the journey and its adventures might be thought
to constitute an ironic reflection on the relative mediocrity of
our daily lives.) Bernard's desire, as he confides to Laura, is
to 'rendre un son pur, probe, authentique' (p. 198). Both
Bernard and his creator appreciate the difficulty of the task.
There appear to be no models for guidance, and Bernard's conclusion is that 'presque tous les gens que j'ai connus sonnent
faux' (p. 198). The chief obstacle to the individual's quest for

authentic self-realization was, in Gide's opinion, the constraints exercised by the family cell. 'Familles, je vous hais', Ménalque had cried in *Les Nourritures terrestres,* and Gide's distaste for the family unit is again patently clear in *Les Faux-Monnayeurs.* Bernard, however, holds a trump card in the Gidean view of life: he occupies a privileged position by virtue of being a bastard. The bastard had featured in many of Gide's earlier works and was for him a means of enjoying vicariously the freedom his personal situation denied him. It is no coincidence, for example, that his fascination with the ideal of the *acte gratuit* is given its most thorough exploration in *Les Caves du Vatican* through Lafcadio, the most colourful of all his bastard-figures. Edouard, moreover, would appear to be acting as Gide's spokesman when he notes: 'L'avenir appartient aux bâtards — Quelle signification dans ce mot: *"Un enfant naturel!"* Seul le bâtard a droit au naturel' (p. 113). In the course of an illuminating survey of Gide's literary bastards, D. A. Steel provides a helpful summary of the attractions for Gide of the illegitimate hero:

> It is the bastard who, on Gide's behalf, throws off the yoke of the family from the shoulders of the individual. In doing so, he becomes the individual who finds and expresses his hidden, divine self. Indeed, by metaphorical exaggeration, he becomes at times divine. He wrestles with an angel as does Bernard the bastard in *Les Faux-Monnayeurs.* He appears in the person of Theseus as a Greek god. He becomes the ideal individual as Gide saw him (*38,* pp. 239-40).

Bernard has much in common with at least one of his predecessors: 'Le caractère décidé de Bernard n'est pas sans rappeler, dans les *Caves,* l'esprit d'initiative de Lafcadio: c'est un Lafcadio qui tournera bien' (*22,* p. 282). Both he and Lafcadio:

> display the same wild bravado, both favour a tone of studied insolence in their letters, each commits a voluntary dishonest action that irremediably binds him to his separate fate. They have a subtler kinship in their respec-

tive relationships to their novelist acquaintances Edouard
and Julius. Each has the opportunity of employment as
literary secretary to the novelist. The two novelists indulge in impotent intellectual play with ideas which are
too powerful for them to handle but which the two
bastards will capably convert into action (*38*, pp. 244-45).

It is not surprising, therefore, to learn from the *Journal des
Faux-Monnayeurs* that Bernard's role in the novel was originally to have been filled by a character named Lafcadio.

But if Lafcadio's ambitions remain largely unrealized, Bernard's greater maturity enables him to become something of an
exemplary figure. He is, indeed, as Steel points out, 'Gide's
major and most mature statement of his conception of the
bastard' (*38*, p. 240). Oscar Molinier is right to see within
him 'les fruits du désordre' and 'des germes d'anarchie' but,
unlike Strouvilhou, [4] Bernard exploits only the positive dimensions of his anarchistic bent. Perhaps the narrator is right when,
in his central survey of the characters, he suggests that Bernard's reserve of anarchy has been largely sapped by his initial
act of rebellion. What we see, in contrast to Lafcadio's un-
bridled activity, is Bernard's 'besoin d'ordre contre lequel se
dresse son envie d'émancipation. Tout son itinéraire romanesque
se constituera comme une oscillation entre ces deux pôles' (*18*,
p. 12). Pure anarchy is a self-denying activity running counter
to the essential Gidean ambitions. Self-realization has to be
more of a dialectical activity in which the constraits wielded
by the family and society are not banished by individualistic
acts but are accepted as being in a dynamic relationship with the
demands made by the self. Thus Bernard, rather than pursuing
some pre-established chimerical abstraction, remains open to
all experience and ready to learn from the situations in which
he finds himself.

At this point it becomes necessary to look at Bernard's
progress in slightly more detail. In the course of the novel, the
already mature Bernard, who clearly enjoys the respect of his

---

[4] It is tempting to view Strouvilhou as yet another bastard. No
mention is ever made of his family apart from his cousin Ghéridanisol.

creator, makes a number of discoveries about himself and arrives at a conclusion that bears witness to an even greater maturity. It is, as was stressed earlier, not an easy quest, but the process of learning about society and the nature of his own self is not as anguished as we might have expected. Bernard does not, for example, make as many wrong and painful choices as does Olivier, whose 'progress' provides the obvious point of comparison. What is more, Bernard is endowed with a strong sense of purpose. He knows he has to go it alone and he rejects Olivier's offer of help. He is soon adept at constructing eloquent dialogues with himself and he is not above self-parodic comparisons with Hamlet (he observes ruefully that he cannot afford the luxury of a ghost!) or Theseus.

At the outset, his enterprise would seem to be one of pure experimentation; he is motivated by the vague goal of 'tout oser'. Adventure is enjoyed for its own sake:

> 'Dans un instant, se dit-il, j'irai vers mon destin. Quel beau mot: l'aventure! Ce qui doit advenir. Tout le surprenant qui m'attend.'... Il songe à sa nouvelle règle de vie, dont il a trouvé depuis peu la formule: 'Si tu ne fais pas cela, qui le fera? Si tu ne le fais pas aussitôt, quand sera-ce?' Il songe: 'De grandes choses à faire'; il lui semble qu'il va vers elles. 'De grandes choses', se répète-t-il en marchant. Si seulement il savait lesquelles! (p. 59).

His prevailing spirit declares itself to be one of scepticism: 'C'est au point que je doute si l'on ne pourrait prendre le doute même comme point d'appui; car enfin, lui du moins je pense, ne nous fera jamais défaut. Je puis douter de la réalité de tout mais pas de la réalité de mon doute' (p. 292). By the time he comes to write his baccalaureate essay on La Fontaine, he is however ready to criticize 'l'esprit d'insouciance, de blague, d'ironie' which together make up 'l'esprit français'. In his view, 'le véritable esprit de la France était un esprit d'examen, de logique, d'amour et de pénétration patiente' (p. 257). But the turning point in his development is of course his extraordinary struggle with the angel and his subsequent return to the family.

The episode with the angel — a deliberate echo of Jacob's struggle with the angel as told in *Genesis* (cf. *4,* pp. 219-20) — was much disliked by Martin du Gard, and as a device it may indeed be open to criticism, but its function is clear. It dramatizes the ascendancy that is gradually being assumed by the better side of Bernard's nature. Long past is the straightforward thirst for adventure. Having been thwarted in his desire to fulfil a useful role as Edouard's secretary, Bernard is even more anxious to make a contribution to the world. However, his continuing development becomes possible only when he has understood that true self-realization cannot be achieved outside a relationship: 'Il commençait à comprendre que le bonheur d'autrui fait souvent les frais de l'audace' (p. 337). His self-questioning, which he continues *viva voce* in the presence of Edouard, reveals unambiguously the direction of his newly formulated quest:

> Pour se diriger dans la vie, est-il nécessaire de fixer les yeux sur un but?... A quoi faire servir cette force que je sens en moi? Comment tirer le meilleur parti de moi-même? Est-ce en me dirigeant vers un but? Mais ce but, comment le choisir? Comment le connaître, aussi long-temps qu'il n'est pas atteint? (p. 338).

Servir and *s'offrir* are the key verbs. The difficulty of the task they imply is, however, emphasized by the superficially attractive doctrine of service and self-sacrifice glorified by the *Action française* (or similarly right-wing and nationalistic) meeting to which the Angel takes him. Bernard has to realize not only that the doctrines of Maurras and Barrès are a pernicious influence on society but that they are also in complete conflict with the laudable desire for self-realization. Gide's message seems clear: a political philosophy based on the total subordination of the individual to the discipline of party or state will lead, at the very least, to atrophy; the well-being of society depends on the encouragement of the individual's authentic growth as a social being. Once Bernard has resisted the temptation to sign his allegiance to the party, he is led into a world hitherto unknown to him: 'Puis l'ange mena Bernard dans de pauvres quartiers, dont Bernard ne soupçonnait pas auparavant la misère. Le soir tombait. Ils errèrent longtemps entre de hautes maisons sordides qu'habitaient la maladie, la prostitution, la honte, le crime et la faim' (p. 335). As his subsequent actions show, the lesson here is one of charity and compassion. Bernard's is 'une nature généreuse' and he needs the opportunity to put this *générosité* into practice. His final return to his family is often seen as a defeat but this is far too simple a reaction. What makes him go back is very largely compassion for his 'father'. (As Edouard observes: 'Bernard n'a plus écouté que son cœur' (p. 378).) The very positive lesson he has learned is given a clear formulation: 'Il n'y a pas de plus grande joie que de réjouir un autre être' (p. 331). Many readers of *Les Faux-Monnayeurs* have stressed only the negative aspects of Gide's treatment of love. These are undeniably important but a case can, I think, be made for seeing love as a vital factor in Bernard's progress towards self-realization. His contrasting experiences with Laura and Sarah enable him to distinguish between generous and ignoble sentiments. It is not fortuitous that the crisis-point represented by his struggle with the Angel follows closely upon the termination of his unfulfilling relationship with Sarah. His return to the fold (Gide had already used the parable of the prodigal son in a text of 1907) is therefore not to be taken as evidence of Gide's unrelieved pessimism. It is, rather, a clear sign of a realist's approach to life. Bernard is a social being and cannot survive outside society. When he goes back to the Profitendieu family, it is far from being a return to square one. (It should be noted that Laura and Madame Profitendieu also return to the family cell.) What he has learned *en route* should enable him to seek fulfilment through the balancing of the conflicting aims and pressures he feels rather than through attempts to satisfy goals that, on closer inspection, reveal themselves to be vague abstractions.

Thus if *Les Faux-Monnayeurs* is in many ways an open-ended novel, Bernard's voyage of self-discovery seems to contain an implicit but nevertheless unequivocal message. The conversation between Bernard and Edouard in Chapter 14 of Part III provides further commentary on the most desirable course of action for the being in search of fulfilment. Above all, however, it shows that the existence of a clear message from the author does not mean that the problems of the individual are resolved once and for all. A leap of faith is required, and uncertainty will never be banished. As Bernard says: 'Si encore j'étais certain de préférer en moi le meilleur, je lui donnerais le pas sur le reste. Mais je ne parviens pas même à connaître ce que j'ai de meilleur en moi' (p. 339). Edouard admits that he has no concrete advice to offer: 'Vous ne pouvez trouver ce conseil qu'en vous-même, ni apprendre comment vous devez vivre, qu'en vivant.' To Bernard's understandable objection 'et si je vis mal, en attendant d'avoir décidé, comment vivre?', he replies: 'Ceci même vous instruira. Il est bon de suivre sa pente, pourvu que ce soit en montant' (p. 340). The vagueness of such advice should come as no surprise. The beliefs on which the novel is founded would be betrayed by a programme that was any more specific. None the less, it is sufficient to look back at Bernard's original attitudes to realize how much progress he has made.

So far, I have stressed that Gide's indictment of society is conducted largely in terms of the widespread lack of sincerity he discerns in the behaviour of individuals. There are, however, signs in the novel of his hostility to certain very precise examples of political behaviour. Just as the activities of the literal *faux-monnayeurs* flit menacingly in the background, so an unmistakable current of what may broadly be described as 'fascism' is often fleetingly encountered when characters take a step outside the narrow world of their personal and family relationships. It may be a discreet presence but it is all the more dangerous for that. Although the only political event of any substance depicted in the novel is the deplorable meeting at which Charles Profitendieu, but not Bernard, pledges his support for the party's right-wing principles, a copy of *Action française* is read by one of the students in the Luxembourg Gardens, and passing reference is made to the electoral career of Barrès. Strouvilhou's eugenics echo Vincent's botany lesson on selective breeding. Moreover, it is the members of the *Confrérie des*

Hommes Forts who exclude Boris and prey upon his weakness. As for Lady Griffith, her exhortation to Vincent continues the Nietzschean ethic of the 'superman' that, in its debased form, is often at the basis of the fascistic tendencies so far mentioned: 'J'abomine les médiocres et ne puis aimer qu'un vainqueur. Si tu veux de moi, que ce soit pour t'aider à vaincre' (p. 66). So crowded are the themes of *Les Faux-Monnayeurs* that this political theme may all too easily escape the attention of the reader who is busy attending to other matters. Yet there is good reason to suppose that Gide attached some considerable importance to his depiction of the threat of fascism. In the thirties he was to become a prominent anti-fascist, and for a brief period he saw the Soviet Union as a model state. (A visit to Stalin's country in 1936 caused him to return disillusioned and highly critical of the regime, not least as a result of the Party's persecution of homosexuals, but principally because his character was naturally opposed to any form of totalitarianism. See his essay *Retour de l'URSS*.)

On occasion, the honest soul in the world of *Les Faux-Monnayeurs* will come face to face with an even more redoutable enemy than any of those previously outlined: Evil and its agent, the Devil. For although the dividing line between hypocrisy and evil in this novel is extremely thin (and there is more than one hint that the right-wing sentiments to which I have just referred are meant to be seen as evil), certain manifestations of evil that are to be found here cannot in all honesty be given another name. Of these the most obvious is clearly the death of Boris. The supreme importance of this event was recognized by Gide himself in a letter he wrote in July 1939 in reply to a young critic, Jacques Lévy: 'Dès cette phrase de votre lettre initiale: "L'atrocité de la mort de Boris me semblait *un crime collectif pesant sur tous les personnages;* elle révèle leur solidarité et donne son sens au titre de ce livre", je me suis senti le cœur gonflé de reconnaissance: oui, c'est bien là ce qu'il fallait comprendre. C'est la clef du livre, la clef de voûte; tout y aboutit' (*28*, p. 36. See also *3*, I, p. 269). A careful reconstruction of events indeed shows just how many characters, wittingly or unwittingly, have hastened the death of a victim who himself accepts his fate with spine-chilling resignation.[5] Edouard terms Boris's death 'suicide', but the reader, who is in full possession of the evidence, will find it difficult to reach such a straightforward verdict. For Gide, then, evil is a force to be reckoned with. Unfortunately, there are many who refuse to struggle against it. On the one hand, there are those, like Azaïs, who refuse to countenance the possibility of evil actions. At the end of the novel, no-one is in fact prepared to suspect Ghéridanisol of such a terrible crime: 'On préfère tout soupçonner, plutôt que l'inhumanité d'un être si jeune' (p. 375). On the other hand, there are those, like Strouvilhou, whose recognition of the omnipresence of evil leads them to accept it almost as a mystical force — Strouvilhou insists that he is an idealist — on which to base their philosophy of anarchism.

In *Les Faux-Monnayeurs* the devil is never far away. Talking of his projected characters, Gide declared: 'J'en voudrais un (le diable) qui circulerait incognito à travers tout le livre et dont la réalité s'affirmerait d'autant plus qu'on croirait moins en lui' (*1*, p. 32). In the eyes of one critic, the devil is actually 'le sujet central':

> non plus le motif, ni le personnage, ni même le thème, car le diable est plus que tout cela. Il est un "principe", comme aurait dit Balzac, principe d'action ou du moins de gravitation, qui, sitôt qu'on le découvre et qu'on l'accepte, ne fût-ce qu'un instant, rend compte de tout l'inexplicable, de tout l'incompréhensible, de toute l'ombre de la vie (*32*, p. 173).

The devil in human form was originally to have been played by Passavant but in the event it is the sinister Strouvilhou whose evil influence lurks in the background. He is, in the words of Lévy, 'un personnage invisible que nous suivons à la trace, et qui prend de plus en plus d'assurance, et qui finit par apparaître en corps' (*28*, p. 75). He controls Ghéridanisol and masterminds

---

[5] There is none the less a danger in apportioning blame too readily. Can Edouard really be held responsible for Laura's pregnancy by Vincent? (Cf. *42*, p. 356).

the activities of the counterfeiters. His name appears on the hotel register at Saas-Fée, and it is he who takes possession of Boris's talisman. Yet Strouvilhou is far from being the novel's only manifestation of the devil. It is the devil who moves Bernard to revolt, and at one point he provides him with a necessary coin. 'Le diable amusé' watches Vincent enter Lady Griffith's house. Olivier's jealousy on reading Bernard's letter causes him to give refuge to the Devil. ('Cette nuit, les démons de l'enfer l'habitèrent' (p. 171).) The natural scientist Vincent falls victim to his inability to believe in the Devil: 'La culture positive de Vincent le retenait de croire au surnaturel; ce qui donnait au démon de grands avantages' (p. 141). (Baudelaire had already claimed that 'la plus belle des ruses du diable est de vous persuader qu'il n'existe pas'.) So vulnerable, in fact, is Vincent as a materialist that he ends up mad, thinking he is himself the Devil. La Pérouse, on the other hand, concludes that God and the Devil are identical; it is indifferent to him whether the cruel treatment he receives stems from one or the other.

It is one thing to recognize the omnipresence of Gide's Devil, it is quite another to identify his status or significance. At the very least, the Devil's role is a teasing one in this novel, and it is small wonder that Gide's use of *le Malin* has often been found less than satisfactory. For some years before *Les Faux-Monnayeurs,* he had been declaring himself preoccupied with the Devil. A conversation with Jacques Raverat, recorded in *Feuillets,* led him to realize that the Devil was not to be seen as a metaphysical entity 'fait du défaut du bien': 'Le mal est un principe positif, actif, entreprenant' (*OC,* VIII, p. 349). The discovery was a revelation: 'Je n'eus pas plus tôt *supposé* le démon, que toute l'histoire de ma vie me fut du même coup éclaircie' (ibid., p. 351). The reader is bound to ask, however, whether Gide is here referring to a Christian concept. And to no avail. Not only does Gide leave this question unsettled, he adds the following, disconcerting note: 'il m'est complètement indifférent, ensuite, que ce nom de démon, soit ou non, le vrai nom de ce que je veux dire, et j'accorde que je le nomme ainsi par commodité; si tel vient ensuite me montrer qu'il n'habite point les enfers, mais son sang, mais mes reins ou mon insomnie, croit-il ainsi le supprimer?' (ibid., p. 351). When it comes to *Les Faux-Monnayeurs,* it is clear that Gide is in part using the devil as a literary device, 'a shorthand way of imparting to the character certain realizations, without the need to invent a series of time-consuming educative experiences' (*45*, p. 93). As such, his devil is part of a line that stretches back from Dostoevsky to Blake and Lesage. Of these, Dostoevsky was clearly the most important to Gide, [6] and it has been claimed that 'one senses at times that the Frenchman felt he *had* to believe in the objective existence of "the Adversary" because Dostoevsky has made it credible, somewhat as a young Frenchman traveling in Scotland feels he must believe in ghosts, because he has read ghost stories located in Scotland'. [7] At times, moreover, the devil in *Les Faux-Monnayeurs* seems little more than a figure of speech, at others part of a dialogue with the self, and more particularly a metaphor for the unconscious: 'Il accompagne dans l'œuvre de Gide la diffusion des travaux de Freud, incarnant le travail de l'inconscient, les pulsions de la libido, la puissance de vie qui pousse à la curiosité, à l'ouverture, à l'aventure, en opposition aux forces d'emprisonnement et de répression' (*18*, p. 26, n. 8). He has also been seen as a relative of Goethe's Mephistopheles and, as such, in possession of a strongly creative force. [8] But it is none the less largely as a tempter, though not necessarily a being external to the individual, that he is presented to us. And for Gide temptation consists largely of a pressing invitation to follow one's own desires. The devil is thus a personal demon who whispers: 'Consens à appeler nécessaire ce dont tu ne peux pas te passer' (*OC,* VIII, p. 348). If

---

[6] *Les Faux-Monnayeurs* was written under the sign of the Russian novelist, and it would appear that Gide's original aspiration was to make the novel resemble Dostoevsky's work still more closely; though, as his highly Gidean lectures on the Russian show, it seems unlikely that he could ever have reproduced the true spirit of Dostoevsky's writings. (Cf. *4*, pp. 26 & 34.)

[7] Henri Peyre, *French Literary Imagination and Dostoevsky and Other Essays* (Alabama, University of Alabama Press, 1975), p. 12.

[8] See Renée Lang, *Gide et la pensée allemande* (Paris, Egloff, 1949), p. 167.

he possesses an infinite stock of seductive arguments, it is, as Dostoevsky had already shown, because he occupies the very seat of our intellect, our powers of rationalization ('c'est surtout dans le raisonnement qu'il se cache'), and Gide adds: 'Si nous étions plus humbles, c'est lui que nous reconnaîtrions dans le *Cogito ergo sum.*' (See also the fifth of the lectures Gide gave on Dostoevsky in 1922 (Plon, 1923; Gallimard, *Idées,* 1964).)

In view of the repeated emphasis on the devil in both *Les Faux-Monnayeurs* and elsewhere in Gide's writings, it is difficult to dismiss Gide's *Malin* as a convenient device. Yet it is impossible on the basis of these writings to come to any conclusions about Gide's theological position, even in the most general terms of whether or not he believes in the supernatural. It is impossible to draw 'a hard and fast line between moral concern and literary preoccupation, between spiritual torment and intellectual play' (*45,* p. 96). [9] What can be affirmed, however, is Gide's insistence that we should be alive to the blandishments of an active evil force that is no less real for ultimately being of uncertain origin. Uncertainty may be thought to be of the essence of such forces, and it is wholly characteristic of Gide to suggest certain alternative ways of viewing the devil without imposing on us a conclusion of his own.

Henri Massis made much of these aspects of Gide's novel, claiming: 'C'est le problème du bien et du mal, la notion du péché, qui est l'obsession de son œuvre.' [10] The indisputable presence of Evil and the devil indeed suggests that it is not just the particular organization of society that is to blame for the behaviour that so horrifies Gide. Moreover, one of Vincent's biological discourses, taken together with the cruel anecdote of Lady Griffith concerning the shipwreck of *La Bourgogne,* suggests a highly unflattering view of human nature. The phenomenon of the euryhaline fish, which can survive changes in the saline content of water, preying on the defenceless stenohaline fish, which depend for their survival on water that contains a

---

[9] See also *10.*
[10] Henri Massis, *Jugements,* 2 vols (Paris, Plon, 1924), II, p. 8.

high proportion of salt, can easily be taken as a metaphor for two similar categories of character at large in Gide's world. As in the case of *La Bourgogne*, life is a survival of the fittest, and chance is seen to play its role. C.S. Brosman concludes: 'Gide suggests that... we must see social mechanisms, often masked, against the background of natural ones' (*13*, p. 55. See also *8*, pp. 142-48 and *4*, p. 32). Particularly disturbing in this respect is the spontaneous viciousness and cruelty of the younger children in the novel. It remains unclear whether we may reasonably hope that in some cases they will eventually grow to resemble the more sensitive adolescents, Bernard and Olivier.

From evil and the Devil, it is a short step to the question of Gide's religious beliefs. Religion, as so often in Gide's work, is a fundamental concern in *Les Faux-Monnayeurs*. The impact of his religious upbringing was such that throughout his life he found it natural to express himself in terms of religious metaphors or parables. Yet Sartre felt able to claim: 'Ce que Gide nous offre de plus précieux, c'est sa décision de vivre jusqu'au bout l'agonie et la mort de Dieu' (*37*, p. 88). And religion is revealed not only as singularly helpless in combating evil or hypocrisy, but also to be a major contribution to the ills of society. So great was Gide's concern with the existence of both God and the Devil that many, both then and more recently, have felt that he was on more than one occasion on the verge of belief. But those who have tried to rehabilitate Gide as a Christian writer have, it would seem, often allowed their conclusions to be coloured by their own faith. The record for conversion to Catholicism among the leading writers of Gide's day was impressive, and there is no doubt that more than one Catholic writer looked upon Gide as the prize catch. François Mauriac remembers that 'André Gide s'irritait parfois de sentir autour de lui tous ces chrétiens à l'affût' (e.g. Claudel, Jammes, Ghéon, Copeau, du Bos) (*7*, p. 103). Although there were occasions when they can be forgiven for seeing signs either of a possible conversion or a return to the Protestant fold, in retrospect it is difficult to question Sartre's view of Gide as an atheist, albeit often a reluctant one. As Philip Thody has written: 'Implicit in the character of La Pérouse — the plaything of God — and in the tragedy of Boris's death is the condemnation of God as the greatest coiner of them all' (*41*, p. 354). The status of the devil may be in doubt, and we may expect from this open-ended novel at least an implicit refusal to come to any definitive conclusion on matters concerning the existence of God, but there is little to suggest that religion was for Gide a consolatory or uplifting faith, or a vital corrective to his tendency towards *disponibilité*. It would seem not a little idiosyncratic to adopt Lévy's view of *Les Faux-Monnayeurs* as a Christian novel, with Boris appearing as a Christ-like figure. None the less, it has to be said that it is the Protestant church and its members, rather than religious belief itself, that attracts most of the author's biting criticisms. As was noted earlier, the *Pension Azaïs* and its austere incumbents have a deleterious effect on many if not all of the characters who pass through it. On the other hand, it remains significant that the sympathetic Pauline who, unlike even the misguided drudge Rachel, avoids the author's irony or contempt, is expressly presented as a nonbeliever.

The modern world's answer to religion — Science — scarcely fares any better. Vincent (a parodic Darwin?), we are led to believe, murders Lady Griffith and ends up insane. As for Freudian analysis, which, although not identified by name in the novel, is undoubtedly the doctrine professed by Madame Sophroniska, it receives at best a guarded welcome. Initially, there was much to commend psychoanalysis to Gide. Quite apart from the intrinsic appeal Freud's theories possessed for a man of Gide's intellectual curiosity, they were of obvious interest to him in respect of their emphasis on the formative years of the child. *Si le grain ne meurt* was, it will be remembered, written at the same time as *Les Faux-Monnayeurs,* and although Martin du Gard was to reproach him for his reticence, Gide included in his autobiography several references to his childhood sexual experiences. Readers of the novel have not been slow to point out similarities between the child Gide and young Boris. [11]

---

[11] 'Mon hypothèse est qu'il s'agit dans cet épisode des *Faux-Monnayeurs* d'une sorte de confrontation entre le moi adulte d'André Gide

Thanks to Dr Gourévitch, we now know, however, that for the character of Boris Gide drew extensively on an article by the model for Madame Sophroniska, Eugénia Sokolnicka, in which this Polish disciple of Freud described the master's treatment in 1919 of a ten year old boy from Warsaw. [12] It was particularly the therapeutic side of psychoanalysis that interested Gide, for his own nervous illness had been treated by more conventional means. But, as presented in the novel, psychoanalysis appears singularly powerless to restore Boris to full mental health. It is true that in part the failure might be ascribed to the inadequacy of Mme Sophroniska as a practitioner. She seems to have a blind faith in the new healing; she is guilty of serious professional indiscretion in telling Edouard the intimate details of Boris's illness (but how else could Gide have subjected her ideas to scrutiny?); she plays her part in the death of Boris by giving his talisman to Strouvilhou (is this blunder conceivable in an analyst?); and exhibits a most unscientific leaning towards mysticism, [13] a tendency that leads her to encourage the counter-productive relationship between Boris and Bronja, a relationship that also receives the uninformed approval of Bernard. (Steel notes (*39*, p. 69) that were it not for the orthodox insistence on infantile sexuality, it would be tempting to see Madame Sophroniska as a disciple of Jung rather than Freud.) Thus psychoanalysis is hardly shown off to good advantage by this particular practitioner. If Gide had been more taken with the therapeutic possibilities of Freud's teaching, he could easily have invented a more convincing therapist. The evidence suggests that he had grave reservations about the efficacy of

---

et son moi enfantin ou, plus exactement, entre l'un de ses moi adultes et l'un de ses moi enfantins' (Jean Delay, *La Jeunesse d'André Gide*, 2 vols. (Paris, Gallimard, 1956-57), I, p. 219).

[12] See E. Sokolnicka, 'Analyse einer infantilen Zwangsneurose', *Internationale Zeitschrift für Psychoanalyse*, 6 (1920), 228-41, Michel Gourévitch, 'Eugénie Sokolnicka, pionnier de la psychanalyse et inspiratrice d'André Gide', *Médecine de France*, 219 (Feb. 1971), 17-22, and Steel (*39*).

[13] Edouard shares her appreciation of mysticism: 'Sans mysticisme, l'homme ne peut réussir rien de grand' (p. 201).

the whole Freudian approach. Edouard's scepticism is almost certainly his own: what is there to guarantee the authenticity of the confession the patient makes under analysis? What is there to safeguard against the confession's following lines suggested by the analyst? 'L'analyse psychologique', Edouard says, 'a perdu pour moi tout intérêt du jour où je me suis avisé que l'homme éprouve ce qu'il s'imagine éprouver... Dans le domaine des sentiments, le réel ne se distingue pas de l'imaginaire' (p. 73). He also feels that under Madame Sophroniska's treatment 'la maladie s'est simplement réfugiée dans une région plus profonde de l'être, comme pour échapper au regard inquisiteur du médecin' (p. 206). Steel rightly suggests that psychoanalysis is also at odds with Gide's personal values in that it threatens 'l'intégrité du moi'. Gide may have been 'assez impressionné' by Madame Sokolnicka's lectures on infantile sexuality but it would appear from the record kept by Maria van Rysselberghe that the enthusiasm for her ideas in the Gidean entourage was at best muted. [14] And in a diary entry for 1924 we find Gide describing Freud as 'cet imbécile de génie' (*2*, p. 785). He claims to find many of Freud's ideas 'absurd' and questions the doctor's exclusive concern with sexuality. On another occasion he declared: 'Que de choses on affirme au nom de la psychologie! Je crois qu'on peut faire dire n'importe quoi à n'importe qui; c'est la manière qui importe' (*4*, p. 218). The only dimension of Freudianism he appears to appreciate unreservedly is its success in bringing into the open certain hitherto unmentionable subjects. [15]

Boris's *magie* is only one of numerous examples of unsatisfactory sexual behaviour in the novel. In the world of the *faux-monnayeurs*, sex is a recurrent concern, and it is rarely

---

[14] See *4*, p. 121, her comment: 'Quand on pense, comme lui, qu'en psychologie tout reste encore à découvrir, on fait peu de cas de ce qu'on sait déjà' (*7*, p. 164), and Georges Gabory, *Essai sur Marcel Proust* (Paris, Le Livre, 1926), pp. 27-35.

[15] He claimed not to have been influenced by Freud, Dostoevsky or Nietzsche: 'J'ai trouvé chez eux plutôt une autorisation qu'un éveil' (*2*, p. 781). Of Freudianism in particular he wrote (in 1922): 'Depuis dix ans, quinze ans, j'en fais sans le savoir' (ibid., p. 729).

a source of happiness. The many cases of marriage are without
exception joyless affairs. Gide's own *mariage blanc* quite naturally coloured his view of matrimony, and although there had
for a time existed between Madeleine (the Em. of his *Journal*)
and himself a relationship based on friendship and respect, a
crisis had occurred in 1918 which led Madeleine to destroy all
his letters to her. (Prior to *Les Faux-Monnayeurs* Gide claimed
that his work had been written exclusively for his wife. His
novel, he later said, was written for Marc Allégret: 'C'est pour
lui, pour conquérir son attention, son estime, que j'écrivis *les
Faux-Monnayeurs*' (*2*, p. 881).) A sour note on the subject of
marriage found its way into the *Journal* in 1924: 'Tu devrais
te marier. Chercher à faire le bonheur d'un autre être... tu
verrais comme on s'y rend malheureux... tous les deux; oui,
tous les deux. Mais ça instruit' (*2*, p. 791). Not only are the
conjugal relationships in the novel sexually unfulfilling, sometimes causing the partners to seek satisfaction outside the marriage bed, the repressive effect of the Protestant cell leaves
certain characters permanently scarred, in particular the children
of Pastor Vedel. Rachel's self-sacrifice is, like that of Alissa in
La Porte étroite, essentially a denial of her sexuality. Sarah's
reaction takes her close to the opposite extreme. Armand's
behaviour and comments, in particular his perverse desire to
push Bernard into Sarah's bed and his subsequent action with
the bloodstained handkerchief, present a highly disturbing
picture of guilt, shame and inadequacy.

Les Faux-Monnayeurs is also a novel about homosexuality,
and the sympathetic but undramatic portrayal pederasty receives
is undoubtedly one of the book's most original features. Proust
had changed the young men of his life into fictional *jeunes
filles en fleurs*. E. M. Forster's not wholly successful homosexual novel *Maurice* had to wait until the 1960s and its
author's death before it was published. Novels that did treat
the subject tended to be over-insistent in the points they made.
Although some of Gide's readers may consider the instances
of homosexuality to be a further, unwelcome product of a
repressive environment, there is no doubt that, despite Martin
du Gard's attempts to persuade him to leave Edouard's sexuality

in doubt, Gide wanted to make male homosexual love seem a perfectly normal and acceptable fact of life. Edouard's feelings for Olivier are the only expression of tender love in the novel. We may find this tendentious, but tribute must surely be paid to Gide's unhysterical presentation of inversion. In particular, he avoids giving a caricature of the effete homosexual. There is nothing in Edouard's behaviour outside his specific affections and affinities that smacks of his sexual preferences. And by contrasting the bad homosexual Passavant with the good homosexual Edouard, Gide reminds us that conventional morality does not become irrelevant once we are outside the heterosexual world. On the other hand, credulity may be strained when he has Pauline sanction Edouard's love for her son. We may feel that he is, as a result of his own emotional preferences, unable to introduce convincing or interesting female characters. A potential richness is suggested by the range of women portrayed, from the harpie-like Lady Griffith to the saintly Rachel. But they emerge as pale shadows when set alongside the male characters. [16]

Although I had occasion earlier to claim that love played a positive part in Bernard's decision to return to the family, in much of the novel love is seen as a highly problematical state. How can it be otherwise when self-knowledge is presented as an impossible goal, the path towards which is moreover fraught with dangerous illusions and instances of bad faith? Edouard expresses the dilemma lucidly: 'Entre aimer Laura et m'imaginer que je l'aime — entre m'imaginer que je l'aime moins, et l'aimer moins, quel dieu verrait la différence? ... Et, s'il suffit d'imaginer qu'on aime, pour aimer, ainsi suffit-il de se dire qu'on imagine aimer, quand on aime, pour aussitôt aimer un peu moins, et même pour se détacher un peu de ce qu'on aime'

---

[16] A. Clutton-Brock, the *TLS* reviewer of the first English translation of Gide's novel, was of the opposite opinion: 'The older men... are too transparent. But M. Gide's women, especially Pauline... are admirably real, neither too mysterious nor too transparent' (31 May 1928). Mario Praz describes Laura, Pauline and Rachel as 'remote descendants of Sade's virtuous Justine' (*The Romantic Agony*, translated by Angus Davidson (London & Glasgow, Collins, 1966), p. 402).

(p. 74). The loss of self required by love is again a stumbling block for Edouard and many another Gidean character. Significantly, though, Edouard's reflexions are prompted by his relationship with Laura rather than by his relationship with Olivier.

A final theme that follows from the uncertainty of knowledge and therefore from the uncertainty of all moral criteria, is Gide's profound unease with Justice and, more generally, the activity of judging. This was one of his lifelong preoccupations. He had for a fortnight in 1912 engineered for himself a place on the jury at various trials in Rouen and wrote about the experience in *Souvenirs de la Cour d'Assises* (1914). A comment in the opening paragraph of this book provides a clear indication of his attitude towards such proceedings: 'A quel point la justice humaine est chose douteuse et précaire...j'ai pu sentir jusqu'à l'angoisse.' In the 1930s he published two books in a documentary series of crime-dossiers to which he gave the evangelical title *Ne jugez pas*. In *Les Faux-Monnayeurs* the judges play a prominent part, and the suitability of Molinier and Profitendieu to stand in judgment over others is seriously called into question. Insofar as the new generation of lawyers is represented by Charles Profitendieu, the situation is unlikely to see any improvement. But the activity of passing judgment is not confined to the professional lawyers, it is built into the very fabric of the novel, with characters, author and reader being constantly drawn into judgments they are subsequently led to reject.

These, then, are the many varied concerns which receive an airing in *Les Faux-Monnayeurs*. Although it has not been possible to avoid giving some indication of Gide's point of view with regard to these matters, little has been said so far about the treatment these themes receive. This will be one of my tasks in the chapter that follows. It remains here only to recognize that all the themes I have presented relate to a question that Gide felt to be fundamental, that is, the distinction between reality and appearance *(être | paraître)* and the problematical means at our disposal for appreciating the nature of that distinction. This is the ambitious *sujet profond* of the

book, and the opposition between sincerity and hypocrisy is
quite clearly a version in moral terms of the same dilemma.
It is, furthermore, this underlying subject that unites Gide's
consideration of human behaviour with his reflections on the
art of novel-writing. We constantly find that what *Les Faux-
Monnayeurs* has to say about life applies equally well to Gide's
view of art, and vice versa.

3

Interpretations

J'écris, j'écris pour exalter ou pour instruire et j'appelle un livre manqué celui qui laisse intact le lecteur.

(Preface to the definitive edition of *Les Cahiers d'André Walter*)

Parce que "méfiez-vous, dit Diderot, de celui qui veut mettre de l'ordre. Ordonner, c'est toujours se rendre le maître des autres en les gênant". C'est son œuvre que l'artiste doit ordonner, et non le monde qui l'entoure; car l'ordre extérieur rend celui de l'œuvre dramatique impossible.

(Lettres à Angèle)

THERE is no doubt that *Les Faux-Monnayeurs* can, and should, be approached in terms of what Gide and Edouard say about their respective compositions. Indeed, the vast majority of the critical discussions of the novel are based almost exclusively on Gide's own terms of reference, and it has not been difficult for the authors of these studies to find textual examples to illustrate the points they make. Moreover, many of the features I mentioned in the introductory chapter as contributing to the effect of disorientation should by now have revealed themselves to be the product of Gide's conscious intentions. On the other hand, there are, not surprisingly, features of the novel that Gide does not mention. His observations are contained in fragmented jottings, and nowhere does he attempt an exhaustive critical analysis of his text. Not that we should expect him to. None the less, the limitations of Gide's own theory as a key to *Les Faux-Monnayeurs* are very real and stem from the absence of any discussion by him of how

example of Laura may be found helpful. No two indiv-
iew her in the same way. Each conception of her char-
shaped by the role she plays in the life of that particular
r. Yet it is not simply a matter of the observer's inev-
ubjective and partial point of view: Gide rightly shows
part we act according to the role we think others expect
If by the end of the novel the reader is slightly perplexed
different pictures he has received of Laura and feels he
ot really got to know her, this does not illustrate incon-
cy in Gide's art of characterization but a deliberate avoid-
by him of a single, privileged viewpoint. Like all human
s, Laura will in some ways remain hidden from both
lf and others. Further consideration of individual char-
s would reveal significant areas of uncertainty, and it is
urprise that those who inhabit the world of *Les Faux-Mon-
eurs* are frequently unhappy with the way they are viewed
others.

The extent to which Gide is successful in making his char-
ers appear to act independently of their author is, however,
en to debate. On several occasions, the authorial voice de-
ares either that it is ignorant of the actions of a character
that it is surprised or disappointed by their behaviour. In
articular, the narrator's remarks in the final chapter of the
aas-Fée section are meant to imply that his characters possess
very high degree of autonomy. From one point of view such
claim is patently absurd. The characters are the author's
creation and he can obviously make them behave as he thinks
fit. Seen in this light, the protestations of ignorance — 'J'aurais
été curieux de savoir ce qu'Antoine a pu raconter à son amie
la cuisinière; mais on ne peut tout écouter' (p. 30) — may appear so much coquetry. And there is no doubt they are to be
seen as contributing to the deliberately 'self-conscious' dimension of the novel. But they are perhaps not to be categorized
in so neat a fashion. It is, after all, true that the author is not
free to treat his characters in a cavalier fashion; a display of
omniscience would run counter to the impression of spontaneity
and naturalness that forms a large part of the novel's *raison
d'être*. Indeed, whatever reservations we have subsequently, it

the text works. We lack precise remarks about structure, the
'self-conscious' aspects of the composition beyond the basic
idea of the *composition en abyme,* or its deliberate artificiality.
Also, whereas Gide's theoretical ambitions are usually presented by him singly, when they are realized in the text they relate
to each other in ways that are themselves highly significant.
The text has, furthermore, to be seen as the product of a
constant process of relativization, establishing its truths in the
manner of a dialectic and at every level constructed with the
aid of a skilful manipulation of paradox.

Equally, many of the ideas Gide does parade, such as that
of the *roman pur,* receive from him a highly general, not to say
vague, formulation. For it was only through his practice that
he was able to establish his true and often subtle position with
regard to these ideas. So, if we confine ourselves to his own
criteria, we remain in the realm of half-truths, simplifying this
complex work and conveniently ignoring its teasing paradoxes.
Yet when all is said and done, much of the value of analysing
this novel comes as a result of discovering that what we thought
was simple is complex and that what we thought was the whole
truth is only partially applicable. In this chapter, therefore,
I shall be attempting to show both the extent to which *Les
Faux-Monnayeurs* actualizes the experimental ambitions expressed by Gide and Edouard, and the fact that many of the
most crucial features of the text are in their discussions left
unexplained.

There is, I think, a good case to be made for concluding
that Gide has largely been successful in creating an impression of inclusiveness, and in such a way that an impression of
naturalness is produced at the same time. Nearly all the events
touch upon Edouard's life (aged 36, he is situated half way
between the old and the young) and as a result the reader has
the feeling that the account of his life in this period is more
or less complete. The presentation of these events is, moreover, made much more lifelike by virtue of their being freed
from the constraints of a conventional novelistic plot. Gide is
indeed closer than was the naturalist novel to capturing the

way we naturally experience the individuals and events that surround us. The action is non-sequential, broken up realistically into a host of linked but none the less separate adventures (thereby partially realizing the ambition of Jacques Rivière and other members of the *NRF* group for a modern *roman d'aventures*). [1] For all the characters life is experienced as a continual present or, rather, a succession of present moments. The simultaneity of events is further emphasized by Gide's technique of suspending a character's adventure in mid-air, as it were, and passing on to a succession of other individual adventures that are likewise interrupted and temporarily lost from sight.

Another tactic successfully employed by Gide in his quest for naturalness is that of making the narrative style of both the narrator and Edouard for the most part quite unexceptional. Although the Gidean narrator is, on occasion, blatantly 'self-conscious', and although in his narrative events will sometimes appear contrived and indeed far-fetched, his descriptive manner, like that of Edouard, more usually contrasts with the widespread tendency of novelists to exhibit uncommon powers of observation and indulge in formal descriptions that, paradoxically, may have the opposite effect of 'realism', behaving as they do according to the dictates of conventional literary practice. The narrative styles of Gide's novel are indeed characterized by a spontaneity and ordinariness that for much of the time make their narrators appear in this respect little different from any of us when we comment upon and analyze what is going on around us. (If the reader of *Les Faux-Monnayeurs* is rarely able to forget he is reading a novel, it is always for other reasons.) There is, it will be noted, a marked lack of physical description of character or place. In other words, the presentation is, in one important sense, un-literary, a quality for which Gide consciously strove: 'le style des *Faux-Monnayeurs* ne doit présenter aucun intérêt de surface, aucune saillie' (*1*, p. 72).

As for Gide's desire for open-endedness, a satisfying impression of such a state is created on more than one level. ' "Pour-

[1] See Kevin O'Neill, *André Gide and the 'Roman d'Aventure'* (Sydney, Sydney U.P., 1969).

rait être continué..." c'est sur ces mes *Faux-Monnayeurs*', says Ed choice of ending — Edouard expr know young Caloub — is his way o life goes on. The novel has indeed sentence in the way that *Du Côté* other novels are known for the line (A perspicacious critic, Goulet, has Caloub is an anagram of *boucla*! Gide doit pas se boucler, mais s'éparpiller, A more radical representation of the o rience, though, is seen in Gide's depict frequently emphasized in this novel that unstable entity. In the case of both Ed realization leads to a state approaching Edouard says: 'Je ne suis jamais que ce suis — et cela varie sans cesse' (pp. 72 Edouard will concern himself only with chaque être'. Gide's practice shows this to h tion as well. One of his most considerable ac *Faux-Monnayeurs* is to have given the imp of his characters are free to behave in a nu ways. (Where this is not the case, there is caricature for satirical effect.) One of his earli mieux, was quick to grasp our author's origina pect:

> La grande nouveauté psychologique qui vi
> se mettre au travers du romancier, c'est d
> l'acte n'est plus tout, que la souveraineté
> décidément déchue au point de vue de l'exp
> la connaissance intime de l'homme. Rien ne
> plus d'un aussi mince intérêt que ces romans
> commis par hasard et faisant boule de neige
> héros aux pires déchéances ou aux plus surpren
> sites (*6*, p. 91).

But even more than this freedom from a series of relat atic actions, it is Gide's representation of the *elusive* character that warrants our attention.

is, I think, possible to accept that Gide intends us to take
seriously the implicit claim by the authorial voice that the
characters enjoy an independent existence. Once a character
has been introduced into a fiction, he is restricted to behaviour
that relates him to other characters, the plot or plots. As a
result, the text may develop a logic that was not consciously
part of the author's original design. The role played by an
author's subconscious self is yet another factor that allows his
conscious self to maintain a detached view of his creatures.
It is therefore quite feasible that by the median point in the
fiction Gide is surprised at the way both the characters and
his text have developed.

Two passages in the *Journal des Faux-Monnayeurs,* both
written in 1924, provide further illumination of this point:

1. Le livre, maintenant, semble parfois doué de vie propre ; on dirait une plante qui se développe, et le cer-
   veau n'est plus que le vase plein de terreau qui l'ali-
   mente et la contient. Même, il me paraît qu'il n'est
   pas habile de chercher à "forcer" la plante ; qu'il vaut
   mieux en laisser les bourgeons se gonfler, les tiges
   s'étendre, les fruits se sucrer lentement ; qu'en cher-
   chant à devancer l'époque de leur maturité naturelle,
   on compromet la plénitude de leur saveur (*I*, p. 70).

2. Le mauvais romancier construit ses personnages ; il
   les dirige et les fait parler. Le vrai romancier les
   écoute et les regarde agir ; il les entend parler dès
   avant que de les connaître, et c'est d'après ce qu'il
   leur entend dire qu'il comprend peu à peu *qui* ils sont
   (*I*, pp. 75-76).

These reflections should discourage us from accepting absolutely either the total autonomy of the characters or the author's
complete and conscious control over their invention and subsequent destiny. The reality, as the qualified tone of Gide's
remarks shows, is more complex. What he says encourages the
conclusion that he pays particular attention to the initial stages
of his project, allowing directions to suggest themselves, rather
than seeking to contain the fiction within certain preconceived

patterns and categories. (Compare his remark, 'J'ai écrit le premier dialogue entre Olivier et Bernard et les scènes entre Passavant et Vincent, sans du tout savoir ce que je ferais de ces
personnages, ni qui ils étaient' (*1*, p. 76).) This in no way ex-
cludes, of course, the possibility that when he comes to give
expression to the product of his imagination the composition
will be consciously structured and rigorously controlled.

Yet, in the final analysis, what really matters is not the
acceptability of the theoretical position but the *impression* the
reader gains of the relationship between the author and his
characters. The way in which the authorial voice talks of
his creatures in his half-way survey certainly succeeds in creating a distance between them and him, suggesting that they were
'there to get to know' rather than creations of his own invention. Bernard's development in particular has caused the 'author'
to change his attitude. The reader may well find that this change
of heart echoes his own experience of Bernard. On the other
hand, the case of Edouard may perhaps be found less satisfactory. The 'author's' irritation comes as a surprise, and the
device is perhaps Gide's rather clumsy way of differentiating
between himself and a character who constantly threatens to
become the author's self-portrait. (Similarly, is not Gide's criticism of Edouard in the *Journal des Faux-Monnayeurs* inappropriately harsh?) And when he says of Olivier: 'J'espérais
d'Olivier qu'il aurait mieux su s'en défendre' (p. 217), the
paradox is glaring, and it is surely difficult for the reader not
to be reminded that the author could have fashioned Olivier's
character differently. The impression of the character's inde-
pendence of the author may, in other words, often be little
more than skin-deep. Much depends on whether the comments
the 'author' makes here corroborate our experience of the characters in the pages that have gone before. The individual reader
will decide for himself whether the author maintains successfully throughout the novel a state of passive expectancy with
regard to his characters. By themselves these comments do
little to establish the characters' open-ended nature.

It may well be, however, that these comments on his characters betray a still more fundamental concern with the *struc-*

ture of the novel. There is, after all, explicit recognition here
of the problem of taking the fiction forward: Bernard had
hitherto been the centre of action but is now dismissed (unjust-
ifiably?) as 'beaucoup trop jeune encore pour prendre la direction d'une intrigue' (p. 216); having introduced Laura, Douviers, La Pérouse and Azaïs, Gide is obliged to do something
with them; Vincent interests him, and he regrets this character's departure, while doubtless appreciating the difficulty of
bringing him back into his fiction. The crux of the problem lies
in the many parallel strands set up in the first section of the
novel. Although the reader may be aware of the passing of
time, the first section deviates considerably from the practice
of more traditional texts in the absence of a recognizable
central plot that causes the events described to string together
in a linear progression, and is therefore peculiarly static. The
only really dramatic event — Bernard's departure — occurs at
the very beginning, and the authorial voice will indeed later
have cause to regret this as 'un geste excessif'. As for the Saas-
Fée section, the events are motivated by Edouard's promise to
La Pérouse that he will bring Boris back to Paris, an action
that, in the reader's mind, is unlikely to have dominated the
other questions and activities that had previously been introduced. (At the time, it is, of course, impossible for the reader
to appreciate its full importance.) There comes, however, a
point at which exposition has to cease. For there to be some
kind of conclusion, a more prominent narrative thread has to
coexist with the thematic concerns and the desire to reflect
the randomness of life that are the novel's *raison d'être* in the
first half. The introduction of a unifying linear thread will,
though, inevitably clash with Gide's desire for an open-ended
composition. So at this point in the novel — whether it is during the writing of the novel or at the planning stage is im-
material — Gide comes face to face with some highly thought-
provoking questions concerning its structure. Some kind of
compromise was essential. And the continuing predominance
of theme over plot is made possible only by introducing such
an unexpected and melodramatic conclusion as Boris's suicide,
an act for which only minimal preparation is required.

In other words, what Gide is recognizing here is not so much the anarchic behaviour of his characters or the need to reflect the randomness of life, as the internal difficulties of a composition that is trying to reconcile a new respect for the open-endedness of all experience with a desire to preserve some of the traditional features of the genre, including the need to convey the reader's interest to a point recognizable as a climax or conclusion. Rather than grappling with the infinite potential contained within his characters, Gide is in fact confronted here with constraints that limit his ability to do so. In noting this, we are beginning to realize the inadequacy of Gide's categories for a full understanding of his text.

If the fact remains that Gide has often managed to create an impression of spontaneity and naturalness, such impressions are, paradoxically, the product of carefully planned structures. When attempting to follow the proliferation of strands in Gide's novel, the reader may not always be aware of this fact but a close examination of the text reveals beyond all doubt the highly conscious nature of this composition. (In considering this paradox we shall be led into what is probably the most important of those aspects of the text that are left unmentioned in the theories of either Gide or Edouard.) There is everywhere discernible a tight control over the novel; it is an intellectual game in which the author is more concerned with the significance of the actions presented and the way they interrelate than with exploiting the rich suggestiveness of the situations he has devised. Not only is there the amazing way in which all the characters' destinies become entwined, Gide resorts to the most unlikely of coincidences in order to preserve a tightly circumscribed and unified world. Also to be appreciated is the basic symmetry of the text. It is unlikely to be coincidence that the novel's central section of seven chapters is flanked by sections which both contain eighteen chapters, though it must be admitted that the wise decision to divide the novel into three sections was implemented only when the text was almost complete. (Goulet, in his *décryptage systématique,* has seen this structure pre-figured in the clock on the Profitendieu mantelpiece, which has a candle-stick on either side!) And despite the lack of a prominent plot, in retrospect everything can be seen to lead to Boris's death.

As for the names Gide gives his characters, they are always chosen with care, revealing his delight in deliberate artificiality. The choice of Edouard's name was almost certainly dictated by its original meaning of 'guardian', and Olivier's name is, not inappropriately from Edouard's point of view, a symbol of peace. (Passavant wants to call him Olive!) The names Sarah and Rachel reflect the pious leanings of their parents. Laura, the object of heterosexual love, was perhaps so called in preference to the French *Laure* in memory of the lady Petrarch had addressed in his sonnets (but see also the discussion of Bernard below). In view of his later career, Vincent's name is clearly ironic, while Strouvilhou's Christian name, Victor, is, in view of his diabolic function, frankly ominous. La Pérouse is also the victim of the author's irony, for unlike the famous sailor immortalized by Diderot, he never ventures far from home and sends Edouard to Saas-Fée on his behalf. The author's view of the smug and hypocritical bourgeoisie is admirably summed up in the name Profitendieu, while Passavant makes the reader think either of 'passe avant' or 'pas savant' (the ancestral war cry of Proust's Baron de Charlus). On the French ear the name Lady Griffith will probably have an effect not experienced by the Anglophone, the word *griffes* being admirably appropriate to her function in the novel. (A more esoteric interpretation of her forename has been suggested by Ben Stoltzfus, who notes that Lilian is 'an extension of Lilith, the she-devil of Talmudic lore'.) [2] In the case of Molinier, Strouvilhou and Ghéridanisol, various attempts have been made to see reflections of meaningful near-homonyms but here scepticism is, I think, permissible. *Ghérida* is, however, a near-anagram of Radiguet, and it is generally accepted that Gide had that literary *enfant terrible* in mind, when he came to baptize Strouvilhou's cousin. The most interesting case by far, though, is that of Bernard.

[2] Ben Stoltzfus, *Gide's Eagles* (Carbondale & Edwardsville, S. Illinois U.P., 1969), p. 128.

It has been shown beyond all reasonable doubt (by Goulet) that Gide was here thinking of St Bernard of Clairvaux. He had read, in 1917, Bossuet's *Panégyrique de Saint Bernard,* and a trace of his reading remains in Bernard Profitendieu's words to himself at the end of chapter 6 of Part I (themselves an echo of Virgil): ' "Bernard! Bernard, cette verte jeunesse...", comme dit Bossuet.' Silviano Santiago has also pointed out that the first mention of Bernard in the *Journal des Faux-Monnayeurs* is dated 20 August 1922. It was on 20 August 1090 that St Bernard was born, and the Catholic Church celebrates his feast on that day. (Bossuet's panegyric was uttered in Metz on 20 August 1653.) It is possible to explore the allusion still further. The *Encyclopaedia Britannica* shows that Gide's choice of saint was highly apt in a novel about adolescence, for it tells us that Bernard is to be remembered for his 'intense love-affair with Godly wisdom', his 'impulsive temperament' and 'his ardent zeal'. At one point in his sermon Bossuet indeed recalls the time when the Saint was 22: 'Vous dirai-je en ce lieu ce que c'est qu'un jeune homme de vingt-deux ans? Quelle ardeur, quelle impatience, quelle impétuosité de désirs? Cette force, cette vigueur, ce sang chaud et bouillant, semblable à un vin fumeux, ne leur permet rien de rassis ni de modéré.' [3] As for Bernard Profitendieu, Gide makes much of his youthful impetuosity and devotion to an ideal. The importance of love in the prodigal's return to the fold has already been stressed; his name is once again appropriate, for one of the Saint's favourite prayers ran: 'Whence arises the love of God? From God. And what is the measure of this love? To love without measure.' The return to the family indicates also that the stage of adolescent rebellion cannot continue indefinitely; if Bernard had continued his quotation from Bossuet, this is what the reader of *Les Faux-Monnayeurs* would have read: 'Bernard, Bernard, disait-il, cette verte jeunesse ne durera pas toujours: cette fatale heure viendra, qui tranchera toutes les espérances trompeuses par une irrévocable sentence; la vie nous manquera, comme

[3] Bossuet, *Oraisons funèbres panégyriques* (Paris, Garnier, 1950), pp. 287-314 (p. 296).

un faux ami, au milieu de nos entreprises. Là tous nos beaux desseins tomberont par terre; là s'évanouiront toutes nos pensées.'[4]

Further evidence of this *rapprochement* is hardly necessary but we are indebted to Goulet yet again for drawing our attention to Albéric, a contemporary of St Bernard's, who was subprior at Cluny and Abbot of Vézelay before joining with Bernard to fight the Second Crusade. Both were reformers, Albéric initiating the Cistercian reform at Vézelay and Bernard at the austere Abbey of Cîteaux, which had been founded precisely in order to combat the laxness at Cluny. It was, then, with the former in mind that Gide chose, ironically, to baptize Bernard's 'father' Albéric.[5]

The Saint was not, however, the only model for Bernard. His struggle with the Angel is clearly meant to recall the account of Jacob and the Angel in *Genesis,* xxxii. As Goulet says, the name Profitendieu is 'une version quelque peu parodique d'Israël' ('he that striveth with God'). Also, after his struggle with the angel, Bernard meets Rachel who persuades him to leave Sarah and the Pension Vedel and return home. This is again a Biblical echo: Jacob's struggle was followed by his reconciliation with Esau, in which he is helped by two women, Lea (compare Laura?) and Rachel!

The artificiality of the text is further apparent from the essentially centripetal principles according to which it is constructed. The characters are thus presented purely in terms of a restricted number of recognizably Gidean preoccupations; beneath the impression of random development, there is a highly economical and schematic network of thematic parallels and oppositions. In other words, for all Gide's deft ability to persuade us otherwise, his are not flesh and blood characters

---

[4] Ibid., p. 298.

[5] The importance St Bernard assumed for Gide can be seen in the following comment: 'La lutte... entre Abélard et Saint-Bernard... ne peut prendre fin qu'avec l'humanité même' (*3,* I, p. 471). Cf. his letter to René Schwob, 26 December 1930 (*Lettres inédites sur l'inquiétude moderne,* edited by Pierre Angel (Paris, Les Editions universelles, 1951), p. 105).

but signifying elements in a very conscious thematic structure. To quote Wylie Sypher: 'Gide has no "characters" in his novel but resolves behaviour and motive into formal relationships; a character is simply the functions of behaviour, the positions from which it falls into adjustments with other characters, whose positions cannot, of course, be determined without calculating multiple arrangements' (*40*, p. 297).

Examination of the theme of sincerity (and the omnipresent activity of counterfeiting) has already shown the extent to which all Gide's characters are viewed in these terms. It was seen also that this theme was part of a wider concern with the problem of reality: 'No matter where we start out from we are continuously brought back to the novel's fundamental theme: the problem of reality. The problem of reality consists of the realist's effort to grasp it, the counterfeiter's effort to dissimulate it, the mystic's effort to ignore it, the neurotic's effort to escape it, and the idealist's effort to sublimate it' (*14*, p. 89). But the centripetal nature of the text is not confined to the central themes we examined in Chapter 2. On many other occasions the reader will encounter parallel events, situations and feelings. [6] Blindness, both literal and figurative, recurs as a leitmotif. Different stances towards suicide are adopted by Boris, La Pérouse, Olivier and Bernard. Embarrassment or a lack of embarrassability are frequently used as moral touch-stones. (See *43*). References to either asphyxiation or respiration are common. Nearly all the characters happen to be novelists, would-be novelists or readers of novels who actively engage in discussions of the genre. (See *33* & *34*). Other examples could certainly be found. What they all show, however, is that almost every detail in the text, however insignificant it may appear, is part of a limited number of themes relating to the most central of Gide's preoccupations. By the end of the novel Gide has carefully incorporated a whole range of positions with regard to these preoccupations. Small wonder that one of the novel's first readers, Daniel-Rops, was led to observe: 'Aucun

---

[6] An exhaustive study of this feature of Gide's novel remains to be written. The reader will find selected examples in *14*.

livre n'est plus conscient, plus volontaire, plus composé, plus conduit' (*5, 23*, p. 21).

This remarkable degree of premeditation and deliberate use of artifice is partly explained by the fact that if *Les Faux-Monnayeurs* was to be a significant work of art, it was necessary for it to be not a reflection of life but a stylization of it, an *ordered* randomness. Thus it was that Gide seems at the outset to have provided his composition with a rigorously tidy thematic infrastructure which was then partially disguised by artfully creating an appearance of untidiness and fragmentation. The reader experiences simultaneously a surface impression of the inchoate and, at first almost subconsciously, through the underlying patterns and recurring preoccupations, an impression of symmetry that becomes ever more apparent as he studies the composition. This second impression is, as we shall see later, crucial, if Gide is to come anywhere near realizing his ambitious ideal of the *roman pur*.

This picture is complicated still further by the fact that if in certain respects Gide endeavours to disguise this use of artifice, on numerous occasions, both through the device of the *composition en abyme* and a 'self-conscious' narrator, he draws attention to the fact that his novel, like all novels, is an artificial creation, concerned with itself rather than with the world outside it. Gradually, too, the reader will become aware of the contrived thematic patterns mentioned above; less blatant a 'self-conscious' device, they none the less arouse in him an awareness of what we may call the text's 'self-reflexivity'.

There are, however, good reasons why these acutely 'self-conscious' dimensions of the novel are not all equally blatant. Had that been the case, they would have run counter to Gide's quest for an appearance of naturalness, which as well as being an aim in itself serves also as a vital stage in his presentation of what constitutes the specificity of a novelistic world. For what interested him above all was the paradoxical relationship between artifice and an appearance of reality. It is important therefore that the reader should first be made to believe in the world the novelist creates and only then be shown the highly conscious and artificial way in which that world has been set up. Only then will he appreciate that in a work of art artifice is not at odds with authenticity. (Gide once said to Jacques Copeau: 'On peut exprimer les sentiments les plus vrais, les plus complexes, les plus humains en se servant d'une forme franchement artificielle, où le besoin de poursuivre une ressemblance n'entraverait pas l'esprit' (*6*, p. 84).) And that any impression of naturalness has necessarily been caused by the skilful manipulation of artificial devices. (It is here that form mirrors content, for in the world of the *faux-monnayeurs* the natural and the false frequently appear indistinguishable. Writing, like every other activity, is seen to be unavoidably false. If Gide's novel is saved, it is only by its conscious recognition of this fact.)

Yet if at certain moments Gide either sustains an illusion or appears to shatter it, these positions are by no means the norm. For much of the time, we are left in an ambiguous realm that reflects by its very ambiguity the specificity of all novelistic worlds. Therein may lie much of the fascination exerted by this text. The composition is, then, simultaneously false and natural. It presents a simultaneous impression of growth and restriction, life and abstraction. Furthermore, it oscillates between the real and the surreal. Unexceptional events in the daily lives of characters whose *état-civil* is instantly recognizable are juxtaposed with remarkable coincidences and happenings that are truly fantastic. Reference was made in the first chapter of this study to the strangeness of both chronology and setting. It should now be clear that the chronological contradictions and the ambiguities in the setting are part of a deliberate strategy. The novel treatment of time gives at one and the same time an experience of simultaneity and temporal progression. (This was something Gide at first thought was impossible. See *1*, p. 15.) Similarly, Gide's handling of setting makes it both banal and highly compelling. It seems likely, too, that all this was part of an attempt to provide what Edouard was seeking in his novel: a powerful expression of the general by the particular.

A similar effect comes from the juxtaposition of imaginary characters and the figure of Alfred Jarry. (The Argonauts' din-

ner was, incidentally, an uncanny foretelling of events at a
dinner held in July 1925 in honour of the symbolist poet Saint-
Pol-Roux. [7]) But the ambiguous status of his fictional world is
highlighted still further by the presence of X and Paul-Am-
broise, both of whom clearly represent characters from life
(Martin du Gard and Valéry) but whose identity is never ex-
plicitly revealed. And by the fact that although *Les Faux-Monnayeurs* is not *un roman à clef,* there exist models for other
characters in the novel. It has already been noted that Madame
Sophroniska was modelled on a Polish disciple of Freud, and
that Ghéridanisol owed at least his name to Radiguet. La Pérouse was based on Marc de LaNux, who had been a pupil
of Liszt. (We may not necessarily agree with Gide when he
says that the piano-teacher fails as a character because he is
too closely modelled on a character from life.) The Pension
Vedel was the product of Gide's personal experience; it has
been claimed that Armand was based on the son of Pastor
Bavretel, who had sisters like Sarah and Rachel and an older
brother who, like Vincent, was a medical student. (In earlier
versions of the novel Vincent was a Vedel.) Gide's cousin Paul
has, however, also been seen as a model for Vincent. For
Dhurmer, Gide apparently took Camille Mauclair, and for
Lucien, Christian Beck, literary figures scarcely remembered
today. It appears also that Olivier has some of the features of
Gide's favourite, Marc Allégret. Boris evidently owes something
to a Russian child Gide had known at school but he is also
reminiscent of Pierre de LaNux. The case of Passavant has,
however, aroused particular controversy. That Gide had Cocteau
partly in mind seems certain; he had been jealous of the atten-
tions Cocteau had shown Marc in 1917. It is generally held that
La Barre fixe refers to Cocteau's first novel, *Le Grand Ecart,*
published in 1923, and it seems likely that if Gide had not
become partially reconciled with Cocteau in 1922, Passavant
would have resembled the latter even more closely and been
made a still less sympathetic figure. Yet when in 1958 Cocteau

---

[7] This has already been pointed out by Joseph Gauthier, 'The Or-
ganic Unity of *Les Faux-Monnayeurs*', *Aquila,* 2 (1973), 260-77.

was asked 'Passavant, est-ce vous?', he replied: 'A peine et en surface. Cela faisait partie de sa [i.e. Gide's] méthode à laquelle on pourrait appliquer la phrase de Nietzsche: "Il ne faut pas cracher contre le vent." '[8] Other models for Passavant have certainly been proposed: Jean Lorrain, Remy de Gourmont and Proust's friend, Robert de Montesquiou.

Thus at every level the world Gide knew and the world he was inventing fused ambiguously in what, for him at least, must have been a fascinating amalgam. Admirers of his novel would claim that as a result Gide and his reader are led to appreciate more fully the distinguishing features of both Life and Art.

So far the 'self-consciousness' of Gide's novel has been seen in terms of drawing attention, through the *construction en abyme,* to his ambitions for the novel and, through all the other 'self-conscious' devices taken together, to the paradoxical relationship between appearance and reality. It remains to consider more specifically Gide's handling of 'self-consciousness', bearing in mind the observation made in Chapter 1 that such devices may, quite rightly, still arouse suspicion. As will be seen, it is necessary in the case of *Les Faux-Monnayeurs* to maintain a distinction between the use of an intervening ('self-conscious') narrator, who is not to be regarded as identical to the author, and the 'self-reflexivity' of the text, which in contrast, can be seen as an expression of the author's ambitions for his novel. (Compare *44.*)

In the manner of much 'self-conscious' writing the interventions by the narrator encourage the reader to think about the way the fiction works and, in particular, about the author's degree of control over his fiction. They are also, in the manner of Fielding and Stendhal, an excuse for the narrator to take a playful delight in his own creation. Yet when Gide's use of an intervening narrator is set alongside earlier 'self-conscious' fictions, it is perhaps bound to disappoint. Nowhere does Gide

---

[8] See J.-J. Kihm, Elizabeth Sprigg & Henri C. Béhar, *Jean Cocteau, l'homme et le miroir* (Paris, La Table Ronde, 1968), p. 180. See also *4,* p. 170.

attempt a significant dialogue with the reader's expectations, such as we find in, say, Sterne's *Tristram Shandy*, and the nature of his themes precludes a sustained and sophisticated use of wit. There can, moreover, be little doubt that most of our exploration of the act of writing is activated by the remarks of Edouard rather than by the behaviour of the intervening narrator. On the other hand, it may not be altogether fair to judge Gide's use of an intervening narrator by the practice of his 'self-conscious' predecessors. Indeed, it follows from the fact that Gide makes only spasmodic use of such a figure that *Les Faux-Monnayeurs* is not designed to rival the masterpieces of that tradition. The 'self-conscious' interventions demand to be seen as only one of various narrative strategies. The principal distinction to be maintained here is that between the main narrative and the narrative contained in Edouard's diary. Comparison of the two will show that Gide has been able to develop within a single composition two very different modes of writing.

Quite apart from the 'self-conscious' interventions, the main narrative, particularly in Part I, is characterized by a certain freedom from the restrictions of straightforward *reportage*. Despite Gide's deliberate use of a language that does not call attention to itself, at different times we find in this narrative theatricality, a disregard for verisimilitude, an excursion into the realm of the fantastic and an abnormally long digression (by Vincent) interrupting the flow of events. These moments are, in fact, simply the most extreme forms of a constant feature of the Gidean narrative voice, as opposed to the voice of Edouard. Even when the narrator stays more firmly within the realm of accepted novelistic practice, a certain jauntiness remains. His characters are treated as marionettes to be manipulated, for all his insistence on their autonomy. He enjoys watching and listening to them in the situations he has devised. And although we can detect affection behind the way he plays with his characters, especially the adolescents, the Gidean narrator stands out by reason of his lack of emotional involvement. In contrast, Edouard's diary presents us with the spontaneous feelings of a man who makes no secret of his highly emotional nature. To read Edouard's diary is thus to be treated to a much more sentimental experience than is ever the case with the main narrative. It is perhaps not surprising that Martin du Gard, despite revising his earlier, unfavourable opinion of the 'self-conscious' intrusions, continued to find Edouard's diary the most satisfactory part of *Les Faux-Monnayeurs*. For in the diary, the narrative is not experienced as a problematical discourse; on the contrary, it is quite unobtrusive, functioning as a seemingly unstylized presentation of events, and the reader is in the process given an intimate acquaintance with Edouard's personality.

These two sharply differentiated narrative styles correspond of course to the divergent directions that much of Gide's literary output had followed prior to *Les Faux-Monnayeurs*. The styles that hitherto had been kept separate in such diverse products as the *récits* and the *soties* are here juxtaposed in a single work. (At one stage, he thought of turning his novel into two separate books 'l'un à la manière de *Paludes,* tout à fait critique et déconcertant, l'autre un roman de vie' (*4,* p. 38).) Both styles undoubtedly held their attraction for Gide, but in each case the existence of the other is incontrovertible proof of their limitations. The 'self-conscious' narration was welcomed as a vitalizing expression of the creative imagination, a delight in the author's Protean potential. As for the confessional style of the *récits* and Edouard's diary, this was appreciated for its ability to capture the intimate feelings of a very human figure, one who often resembled Gide himself. On the other hand, it is not difficult to see the limitations of either narrative. Not only does 'self-conscious' narration exclude the emotional response that Gide felt was natural, it has a tendency to go beyond Romantic irony to threaten the destruction of the fiction that has been so carefully created. In addition, if Gide had committed himself to a consistently 'self-conscious' narrative, this would have thwarted his repeated quest for what he regarded as 'classical' perfection. The alternative strategy, though, could never accommodate the creative energies that Gide felt were vital to the act of self-expression. (One of the most radical differences between Gide and Edouard can be seen in the latter's rather colourless personality.) However much the author's use of irony may inject complexity into the accounts we read in Edouard's *récit*, characters' lives always receive therein a presentation respectful of the traditional categories of the *roman d'analyse*.

The structure of *Les Faux-Monnayeurs* was, therefore, designed in part to allow Gide to oscillate between these opposing narrative styles. Neither narrative strategy is, nor could be, fully exploited, for it is only the *idea* of the respective modes that Gide wishes to bring into play. In an important sense, *Les Faux-Monnayeurs* remains an embryonic structure: 'Il semble que ce soit plutôt une œuvre en marche vers le roman, une création qui se serait arrêtée un peu avant la dernière étape de la progression romanesque' (*22*, p. 278). It should not be assumed, however, that these two modes are juxtaposed merely because of Gide's inability to decide which was more suitable for his story. Their co-existence plays an important part in Gide's search for the *roman pur*. For the inexhaustible richness of the world that is Gide's subject is shown to exist beyond the attempts by these two narrative modes to express it. In other words, it is left to the reader to create a mental image of this world from elements taken from both the narrator and Edouard. Since this image will appear to exist independently of a particular narrative voice, it will to a certain extent escape the omnipresent threat of the counterfeit and exhibit the purity of a world that has yet to know the distortions caused by any attempt to represent it in language. This impression of purity is then reinforced by the text's 'self-reflexivity', its total lack of heterogeneous matter. The ideal of the *roman pur* doubtless presupposes a consistent mode of expression. Such consistency would, however, have been at odds with the Gidean cult of *disponibilité*. *Les Faux-Monnayeurs* must therefore be seen as a compromise solution to opposing demands. It exists to show that a 'pure novel', or at least the Gidean *roman pur*, could be suggested but never given definitive expression.

We may conclude that the 'self-consciousness' of *Les Faux-Monnayeurs* operates at more than one level, with the aid of several distinct devices. Together they ensure that the reader is led constantly to reflect on the nature of the composition, but the full complexity of this paradoxical text will emerge only if these devices are kept separate, and if it is recognized that Gide's novel sets out not just to continue the practices of Fielding, Sterne and Stendhal, but to realize as nearly as possible its author's own unique ambitions. [9]

At first sight, *Les Faux-Monnayeurs* seems to be a novel that contains within its pages many adequate pointers to its own nature, but it should now be clear that the picture presented *en abyme* is somewhat sketchy, merely a starting-point for reflection. Recognition of the role played by conscious artifice and 'self-consciousness' has already indicated the paradoxical nature of Gide's text. But as yet, no explicit account has been given of what Gide himself considered one of the most original features of this work, namely the abnormally active role that has to be sustained by an alert and critical reader. However appropriate the terms in which Gide talks of his novel, the text can never be a straightforward expression of his ambitions, communicated to a passive reader. On the contrary, the value of *Les Faux-Monnayeurs* emerges only when we begin to monitor the activity of reading.

Gide's novel is remarkable for its lack of explicitness. Not only are no conclusions stated, it is often left to the reader even to identify the author's numerous thematic concerns, several of which may escape us on a casual reading. Throughout the work, the reader has therefore to bring out for himself the significance of what is merely implicit in Gide's writing. He is thus invited to embark on an enterprise that involves him in the establishment of connections and in the identification of similarities and differences, both at the level of the theory and practice of writing and in respect of themes. Each aspect of form and content is, for example, presented at various points on scales that run from the positive to the negative and from the

---

[9] Once the close link between 'self-consciousness' and 'purity' has been realized, Gide's choice of *La Double Méprise* as the purest novel he knows may seem less surprising. For it too is a fiction that plays with its own fictional status. (See Robert Lethbridge and Michael Tilby, 'Reading Mérimée's *La Double Méprise*', *Modern Language Review*, 73 (1978), 767-85, and the appendix to *44*.)

literal to the figurative. The importance of the reader's role becomes even more apparent, though, when it is appreciated that it is precisely these connections that are Gide's principal concern. It will doubtless have been observed that our author has neither the space nor the inclination to develop any of the fictional situations he has devised or to discuss in depth the many illustrations they afford of his various themes. He accepts that the lives of his characters are essentially commonplace. What interests him is the way things relate and the changes wrought by different points of view. Ultimately, we might conclude, he is concerned not with the emotional and spiritual lives of his characters but with what they can be seen to represent in a highly intellectual scheme of human behaviour.

The reader's role is, however, by no means straightforward. For although certain connections are easily made and are seen to contribute to the underlying sense of pattern we have already observed, Gide's world is consistently one of appearances and shifting points of view. The reader may well experience the need for certainty and order, but he is everywhere obliged to admit that all conclusions are tentative and eventually undermined by another way of looking at things. Seemingly, the only conclusion he may reach is that the world of *Les Faux-Monnayeurs* is one of unyielding relativism. Moreover, once he has set himself on the trail of the implications of Gide's text, there seems no end to the paradoxes he will meet, by no means all of which were necessarily apparent to the author himself. To almost every question he asks himself about this novel, he has to give both a positive and a negative answer.

It is curious that on a first encounter with *Les Faux-Monnayeurs* many readers may feel that the conscious nature of Gide's composition condemns the reader to a subordinate role. It appears that we are given both a novel and its theory, the writing *and* an explanation of its significance. I hope I have been able to show in this all too brief chapter that such an impression has subsequently to be modified. For it seems to me difficult to deny that it is the reader, and not the novelist, who is led to the more interesting discoveries about the nature of the text. In writing *Les Faux-Monnayeurs,* Gide may have

given shape to at least some of his explicit ambitions but in
the final analysis it might be argued that his principal achievement is to have given us a more positive encouragement to
submit the implications of a fictional text to our own critical
scrutiny than almost any French novelist before Alain Robbe-
Grillet and the other *nouveaux-romanciers* of the post-war
period.

4

Conclusion

COMING to a conclusion, however tentative, about *Les Faux-Monnayeurs* is far from easy. The impossibly ambitious nature of Gide's novel and his inevitable recourse to compromise make criticism easy. On the other hand, appropriate criteria for a judgment of individual features are notoriously hard to establish. As Francis Jammes once noted with reference to *Les Nourritures terrestres*: 'Chacune de tes pensées portait en elle, DIRECTEMENT, sa propre réfutation.'[1] Yet it would be wrong to claim that the critic's hands are tied in every respect. When the novel is viewed as a whole, it is possible to form an opinion of its contribution to the development of the French novel and to enumerate some of the recurrent strengths and weaknesses of Gide's writing.

It would be absurd to deny that *Les Faux-Monnayeurs* has the capacity to make its readers think. But we should, I feel, ask ourselves whether it encourages us to discover truths that are in any way novel or profound. It may be thought that, as Germaine Brée has claimed, 'la pensée, pour lui [i.e. Gide] reste toujours trop générale pour s'individualiser; elle tend vers le lieu commun' (*11*, p. 280). We may feel that Gide shows an obsessive concern with his own self, or that, in comparison with Proust, he seeks above all to justify and gratify himself instead of embarking on a truly illuminating voyage of self-discovery. Thus *Les Faux-Monnayeurs* may present a densely populated world of clearly differentiated characters but it might be objected that we are given none of the rich diversity that we observe in everyday life. According to such a view, the novel

---

[1] Francis Jammes-André Gide, *Correspondance 1893-1938* (Paris, Gallimard, 1948), p. 112.

is dominated by Gide's own personality, the characters being presented solely in terms of a limited number of distinctly Gidean preoccupations. Objection may also be made to a tendentiousness that is at odds with the author's much vaunted commitment to open-endedness. To mention a single example, Gide skilfully presents his fictional world in such a way that the reader may well find himself accepting the superiority of Edouard's homosexual leanings somewhat against his will. Not all Gide's readers will recognize as valid the uniformly pessimistic treatment given love and marriage. How can one avoid the conclusion that Gide is indulging in implausible wish-fulfilment when he makes Pauline sanction Edouard's 'protection' of her son?

We need also to ask whether the impression of superficiality in this composition is totally dispelled by our awareness of its calculated subtlety. It is difficult to be sure that this subtlety is not sometimes an exercise in obfuscation or that Gide's practice does not allow him to shirk vital issues, presenting with sometimes questionable sleights of hand his weaknesses as virtues. For so many of the precepts illustrated by *Les Faux-Monnayeurs* hinge on the impossibility of a particular intellectual, moral or artistic ambition. The relationship between Gide and Edouard may give rise to particular misgivings. While there may be some who, like Edmond Jaloux, regret that Gide did not make his superiority over Edouard an undisputed fact, others may be tempted to assume that by leaving in some doubt the precise distinctions to be drawn between the two, Gide was spared the need to come to terms with himself and his ideas. More than one critic has been moved to complain that Gide is playing an elaborate game of hide and seek with his reader.

At every turn, Gide's strange practice can be justified by the particular needs of his composition but this does not mean that the reader is obliged to accept that the realization of the aims the author has set himself is as worthwhile as the latter would have us believe, however brilliant the stratagems to that end. Speaking more generally of Gide's work, Aldous Huxley (whose novel *Point Counter-Point* (1929) is, incidentally, all too often seen as an English *Faux-Monnayeurs*) once observed that the author had 'refined his work till that rather gross, almost physical quality, which is called life, has been distilled out of it along with other crudities'. [2] Some sympathy may also be found for the view of Henry Bidou, who defined Gide's novel as 'ce cours d'eau faussement libre' (*5*, 21, p. 12).

When it comes to Gide's attempt to rescue the Novel from the impasse in which he felt it was trapped, it is perhaps significant that the post-war *nouveaux-romanciers* have been loath to enrol Gide among their precursors, preferring to derive their experiments from the work of Flaubert, Proust and Raymond Roussel. Seen in the light of the post-war experimentalists and *contestataires,* Gide's novel does little to undermine the conventions on which the 'realist' or 'naturalist' novel had rested. Initially, *Les Faux-Monnayeurs* may thwart the reader's expectations but any questioning of the novel as an adequate means of representation is, it may be thought, severely limited by Gide's over-riding concern with the quest for the *roman pur.*

On the other hand, it is undoubtedly true that *Les Faux-Monnayeurs* is 'déjà un livre de l'impuissance du romancier dévoré par ses problèmes de romancier' (*30*, p. 225), and that as such it has fostered further thinking about a genre which was often felt to be the product of Nature rather than a reflection of the epistemological assumptions of a particular age. It may be true that in the final analysis 'son univers romanesque n'est pas la société humaine, c'est seulement le monde étroit de l'écrivain André Gide', [3] but Gide's ability to embody his preoccupations and attitudes in different fictional characters and to allow them to be reflected in instinctive responses to precise physical settings prevents the novel from being as limited as such a statement suggests. The wider relevance of the fic-

---

[2] Aldous Huxley, *Athenaeum,* 4 July 1919. Cf. his remark: 'At one time or another in the course of his literary career, M. Gide has handled almost every spiritual problem of real and fundamental importance. But he has handled them over delicately, with his finger-tips, so to speak' (ibid., 24 September 1920).

[3] Pierre de Boisdeffre, *Vie d'André Gide* (Paris, Hachette, 1970), p. 14.

tional world he has created is indeed seen in the way the novel questions the moral assumptions of the age in which he lived. Anyway, we should, I think, ask ourselves whether the fact that this novel is to a large extent an expression of the character of André Gide is necessarily a reason for censure. Alongside a certain pessimism, there is present in this novel a humanity, sensitivity and critical intelligence that may well be found appealing. As the Belgian poet and critic Roger Bodart so rightly says: 'Gide écrit non pas pour écrire, mais pour être,' [4] and while his novel obviously demands from the reader a high degree of intellectual participation, we are constantly made aware of Gide's lively personality. The shape of his composition may bring us still further pleasure. We may perhaps also agree with Crémieux's approval of 'l'admirable économie de l'œuvre'.

Much will depend on how we choose to approach *Les Faux-Monnayeurs*. Are we to consider it a completed novel or, in Naomi Lebowitz's words, 'a diagnostic work which concerns itself inevitably with the competition of the possible attitudes and frameworks which could be used by more committed novelistic talents' (*27*, p. 293)? The problem is that Gide wants it to be both of these at once. An ambiguous response may therefore be thought the only one appropriate to this ambiguous composition. Yet to call it a partial failure, as many have done, is perhaps too easy. For it might well be argued that Gide is aware that, in certain respects, it is bound to be a failure. (The criticisms he levels against Edouard suggest also that he is only too aware of his own possible shortcomings.) It seems highly plausible to suggest therefore that he was trying to find out how far he could go in the directions he had set himself, exploring in the process the nature of both the difficulties which faced him and the various achievements that prove possible. Perhaps, paradoxically, he was, though, too successful in creating certain illusions, thereby undermining the attempt to make us reflect on the inevitability of his failure. Yet, however we decide to approach this matter, there can, as we have seen, be no doubt that an assessment of Gide's novel must bear in

---

[4] *Cahiers André Gide*, III, p. 139.

mind its ability to make the reader explore the vast range of complex questions it poses, with a degree of critical rigour that obliges him constantly to reconsider the conclusions he has only just reached.

In the final analysis, much will depend on the temperament of the individual reader. Some will claim that Gide is trying to do too much within the bounds of a single work, thereby making unrealistic demands on his readers. Others will welcome the opportunity to become active and 'self-conscious' readers, and they will reach a conclusion that reflects the perennial fascination this text holds for them. Those of us who belong to this second group would, however, perhaps do well to ponder a recent definition of the literary critic as 'un lecteur perverti'.

Select Bibliography

The following are indispensable for the study of *Les Faux-Monnayeurs:*

1. André Gide, *Journal des Faux-Monnayeurs* (Paris, Gallimard, 1927).
2. André Gide, *Journal 1889-1939* (Paris, Gallimard: *Bibliothèque de la Pléiade,* 1948).
3. André Gide & Roger Martin du Gard, *Correspondance,* 2 vols. (Paris, Gallimard, 1968). (Index published by Susan H. Stout (Gallimard, 1971).)
4. Maria van Rysselberghe, *Les Cahiers de la Petite Dame,* I (*Cahiers André Gide,* IV, Paris, Gallimard, 1974). A faithful record of Gide's conversation by a patient and respectful listener.
5. The *Bulletin des Amis d'André Gide.* Numbers 21-24, 26-27, 29 & 31 contain a wide and extremely interesting selection from the reviews that appeared when *Les Faux-Monnayeurs* was first published.
6. *Hommage à André Gide* (Paris, Editions du Capitole, 1928). See in particular the articles on *Les Faux-Monnayeurs* by Crémieux and Jaloux.
7. *Hommage à André Gide* (Paris, *La Nouvelle Revue Française,* 1951) — in particular the article by André Julien, entitled *'Les Faux-Monnayeurs* et l'art du roman'.
8. *Australian Journal of French Studies,* 7 (1970) is a special number devoted to Gide. It contains a number of articles directly relevant to the study of *Les Faux-Monnayeurs.*

FURTHER READING

9. Bouraoui, H. R., 'Gide's *Les Faux-Monnayeurs:* Hidden Metaphor and the Pure Novel', *Australian Journal of French Studies,* 8 (1971), 15-35.
10. Brachfeld, George I., *André Gide and the Communist Temptation,* (Geneva & Paris, Droz-Minard, 1959). A misleading title. The author's aim is to 'show the permanence of the social concern throughout André Gide's life'. pp. 46-47 are concerned with Gide and the Devil, with particular reference to *Les Faux-Monnayeurs.*

11. Brée, Germaine, *André Gide, l'insaisissable Protée,* 2nd edition (Paris, Les Belles Lettres, 1970). One of the best general introductions to Gide's work.

12. Brosman, Catharine Savage, 'The Relativization of Character in *Les Faux-Monnayeurs', Modern Language Review,* 69 (1974), 770-78.

13. Brosman, Catharine Savage, 'The Novelist as Natural Historian in *Les Faux-Monnayeurs', Essays in French Literature,* 14 (1977), 48-59.

14. Ciholas, Karin Nordenhaug, *Gide's Art of the Fugue. A Thematic Study of 'Les Faux-Monnayeurs'* (Chapel Hill, N.C., 1974). Unduly selective in its approach and examples but recognizes the interdependence of theme and structure in Gide's novel.

15. Fernandez, Ramon, *André Gide* (Paris, Corrêa, 1931). A lively essay that is still worth reading.

16. Forster, E. M., *Aspects of the Novel* (Harmondsworth, Pelican, 1962). The 1927 Clark lectures. See pp. 87-88 & 104-09 for mention of *Les Faux-Monnayeurs.*

17. Freedman, Ralph, *The Lyrical Novel* (Princeton & London, Princeton U.P., 1963), pp. 165-82 are devoted to *Les Faux-Monnayeurs.*

18. Goulet, Alain, 'Lire *Les Faux-Monnayeurs', La Revue des Lettres Modernes,* 439-444 (1975), 9-28. A brilliant interpretative essay. The volume contains five other essays on *Les Faux-Monnayeurs.*

19. Greshoff, Jacques, 'La Structure des *Faux-Monnayeurs', Neophilologus,* 43 (1963), 169-86. Expresses reservations about Gide's achievement.

20. Guerard, Albert J., *André Gide,* 2nd edition (Cambridge, Mass., Harvard U.P., 1969). A thoughtful general study that raises many interesting points.

21. Holdheim, W. Wolfgang, *Theory and Practice of the Novel. A Study on André Gide* (Geneva, Droz, 1968). An illuminating study of Gide's creative imagination, if marred by a rebarbative style and too great a distance from the works themselves.

22. Hytier, Jean, *André Gide* (Paris, Charlot, 1945). An important general study given as a set of lectures. Chapters 7 & 8 are devoted to *Les Faux-Monnayeurs.*

23. Ireland, G. W., *André Gide — A Study of his Creative Writings* (Oxford, Clarendon, 1970). A straightforward descriptive account.

24. Idt, Geneviève, *André Gide: 'Les Faux-Monnayeurs'* (Paris, Hatier: *Profil d'une œuvre,* 1970).

25. Klossowski, Pierre, 'Gide, du Bos et le Démon', *Les Temps Modernes,* September 1950, 564-74.

26. Lafille, Pierre, *André Gide, romancier* (Paris, Hachette, 1954).

27. Lebowitz, Naomi, *'The Counterfeiters* and the Epic Pretence', *University of Toronto Quarterly,* 33 (1963-64), 291-310. A highly perceptive article in which the author is concerned to find out how the text works.

28. Lévy, Jacques, *Journal et Correspondance* (Grenoble, Editions des Cahiers de l'Alpe, 1954). Contains a contentious essay on *Les Faux-Monnayeurs* in which the author proposes a religious interpretation of the novel.

29. Magny, Claude-Edmonde, *Histoire du roman français depuis 1918* (Paris, Seuil: *Collection Points,* 1971). Chapters 8 & 9 are concerned almost exclusively with *Les Faux-Monnayeurs.* The author is often critical.

30. Martin, Claude, 'Gide et le "Nouveau roman" ' in *Entretiens sur André Gide,* edited by M. Arland & J. Mouton (Paris & The Hague, Mouton, 1967), pp. 217-42.

31. Martin du Gard, Roger, *Notes sur André Gide* (Paris, Gallimard, 1951).

32. Michaud, Guy, *L'Œuvre et ses techniques* (Paris Nizet, 1957). Contains two essays on the structure of *Les Faux-Monnayeurs.*

33. Prince, Gerald, 'Lecteurs et lectures dans *Les Faux-Monnayeurs',* *Neophilologus,* 57 (1973), 16-23.

34. Prince, Gerald, 'Personnages-romanciers dans *Les Faux-Monnayeurs',* *French Studies,* 25 (Jan. 1971), 47-52.

35. Santiago, Silviano, 'Fragmento do *Les Faux-Monnayeurs',* *Revista do Livro,* 29-30 (1966), 50-94. An early version of Chapter 2 and part of Chapter 3.

36. Santiago, Silviano, *La Genèse des 'Faux-Monnayeurs'* (Unpublished thesis, Paris, 1968).

37. Sartre, Jean-Paul, 'Gide vivant' in *Situations IV* (Paris, Gallimard, 1964), 85-89.

38. Steel, D.A., 'Gide and the Conception of the Bastard', *French Studies,* 17 (July 1963), 238-48.

39. Steel, D.A., 'Gide et Freud', *Revue d'Histoire Littéraire de la France,* 1977, 48-74. Like the previous item, an excellent article containing much that is relevant to a study of *Les Faux-Monnayeurs.*

40. Sypher, Wylie, 'Gide's Cubist Novel', *Kenyon Review,* 11 (1949), 291-309. An interesting attempt to describe *Les Faux-Monnayeurs* in terms of Cubism.

41. Thody, Philip, *'Les Faux-Monnayeurs*: The Theme of Responsibility', *Modern Language Review,* 55 (July 1960), 351-58.

42. Thomas, D.L., *André Gide — The Ethic of the Artist* (London, Secker & Warburg, 1950). Chapter 13 is devoted to *Les Faux-Monnayeurs* and is particularly sensitive to the moral implications of the novel.

43. Tilby, Michael, *'Les Faux-Monnayeurs.* A Novel about Embarrassment', *French Studies,* 35 (January 1981), 45-59.

44. Tilby, Michael, ' "Self-conscious" Narration and "Self-Reflexivity" in Gide's *Les Faux-Monnayeurs'*, *Essays in French Literature*, 15 (1978), 56-81.
45. Watson, Graeme, 'Gide and the Devil', *Australian Journal of French Studies*, 4 (1967), 86-96.